MEASUREMENT AND GEOMETRY

GLOBE FEARON

Pearson Learning Group

Executive Editor: Barbara Levadi
Editors: Bernice Golden, Lynn Kloss, Robert McIlwaine, Kirsten Richert
Production Manager: Penny Gibson
Production Editor: Walt Niedner
Interior Design: The Wheetley Company
Electronic Page Production: Curriculum Concepts
Cover Design: Pat Smythe

Photo Credit (page 18): Jim Cron/Monkneyer Press

ISBN 0-8359-1555-7
Printed in the United States of America

5 6 7 8 9   08 07 06 05 04

Globe
Fearon

Pearson Learning Group

1-800-321-3106
www.pearsonlearning.com

CONTENTS

TO THE STUDENT

Access to Math is a series of 15 books designed to help you learn new skills and practice these skills in mathematics. You'll learn the steps necessary to solve a range of mathematical problems.

LESSONS HAVE THE FOLLOWING FEATURES:

❖ Lessons are easy to use. Many begin with a sample problem from a real-life experience. After the sample problem is introduced, you are taught step-by-step how to find the answer. Examples show you how to use your skills.

❖ The *Guided Practice* section demonstrates how to solve a problem similar to the sample problem. Answers are given in the first part of the problem to help you find the final answer.

❖ The *Exercises* section gives you the opportunity to practice the skill presented in the lesson.

❖ The *Application* section applies the math skill in a practical or real-life situation. You will learn how to put your knowledge into action by using manipulatives and calculators, and by working problems through with a partner or a group.

Each book ends with *Cumulative Reviews*. These reviews will help you determine if you have learned the skills in the previous lessons. The *Selected Answers* section at the end of each book lists answers to the odd-numbered exercises. Use the answers to check your work.

Working carefully through the exercises in this book will help you understand and appreciate math in your daily life. You'll also gain more confidence in your math skills.

CUSTOMARY MEASURE: LENGTH

Vocabulary

customary units: inch, foot, yard and mile are customary units of length.

inch (in.): $\frac{1}{12}$ of a foot

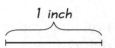

1 inch

This is the length of one inch.

foot (ft): 12 inches

yard (yd): 3 feet or 36 inches

mile (mi): 5280 feet or 1760 yards

Reminder

The remainder in a division problem can be written as a fraction or decimal. Fractions are easiest to understand when written in simplest form.

The peregrine falcon stamp for the United Nations Endangered Species series was designed by Australian Betina Ogden. A peregrine falcon has a wingspan of about $3\frac{1}{2}$ feet. How many inches is that? (A foot is 12 inches.)

Multiply to change from a longer unit to a shorter unit.

$$3\frac{1}{2} \times 12 = \frac{7}{2} \times 12 = \frac{84}{2}, \text{ or } 42$$

$$3\frac{1}{2} \text{ feet} = 42 \text{ inches}$$

The falcon's wingspan is about 42 inches.

A peregrine falcon soars about 270 feet above the ground. How high is that in yards?

3 feet make a yard.

Divide to change from a shorter unit to a longer unit.

$$\frac{270}{3} = 90$$

$$270 \text{ feet} = 90 \text{ yards}$$

The falcon soars about 90 yards above the ground.

Guided Practice

1. Change 15 inches to feet.

a. _____

inches = 1 foot

b. ___*Divide*___ to change inches to feet.

c. $\frac{15}{12} =$ _____ feet

d. 15 inches = _____ feet

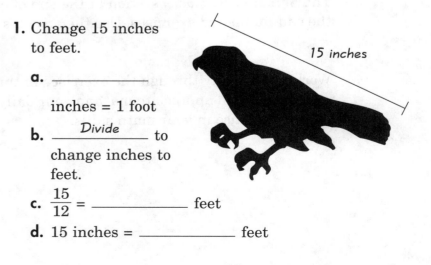

15 inches

2. Change 2.1 miles to yards.

    a. _____ yards = 1 mile

    b. _____ to change miles to yards.

    c. 2.1 × 1760 = _____

    d. 2.1 miles = _____ yards.

Exercises

Change each measurement.

3. 96 in. = _____ ft

4. 12 yd = _____ in.

5. 981 ft = _____ yd

6. 168 in. = _____ ft

7. 1056 ft = _____ mi

8. $\frac{1}{4}$ mi = _____ ft

9. 3.2 mi = _____ yd

10. 1760 ft = _____ mi

11. 8.25 ft = _____ in.

12. $6\frac{1}{3}$ yd = _____ ft

13. 600 in. = _____ ft

14. 720 in. = _____ yd

Application

15. A peregrine falcon hunts by diving, or stooping, at about 924,000 feet per hour. How many miles per hour is that? _____

The whooping crane is the subject of another endangered species stamp. Award-winning artist Norman Adams designed the United Nations whooping crane stamp.

16. The whooping crane's whooping call is so loud, it can be heard up to 2 miles away. How many feet is that? _____

17. Which of the exercises above would you prefer to solve with a calculator, and why?

    _____

    _____

    _____

ESTIMATING LENGTHS IN CUSTOMARY UNITS

Vocabulary

estimate: an approximate measurement. You can use convenient objects and body lengths to estimate lengths.

Sydelle knows that the rim of the basketball hoop is 10 feet from the ground. He estimates that the height of a street lamp is about $1\frac{1}{2}$ times that height. About how tall is the lamp?

Sydelle's **estimating unit** is the height of the basket rim. His **measurement** of the lamp is $1\frac{1}{2}$ times the height of the basket rim.

$$1\frac{1}{2} \times 10 = 15$$

The estimated height of the lamp is about 15 feet.

Guided Practice

Hint

The **measurement** is the number of unit lengths.

1. Walt's hand span is 8 inches. How wide is a display case measuring about 3.5 spans?

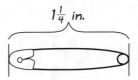

8 inches

   a. The estimating unit Walt is using is ___his hand___.

   b. The unit length is

   _____.

   c. The measurement of the display case is

   _____.

   d. The estimated width of the display case is

   _____.

2. Estimate the length of the line.

   $1\frac{1}{4}$ in.

   _____

   a. The estimating unit is _____.

   b. The unit length is _____.

   c. The measurement of the line is _____.

   d. The estimated length of the line is _____.

Exercises

Complete the table.

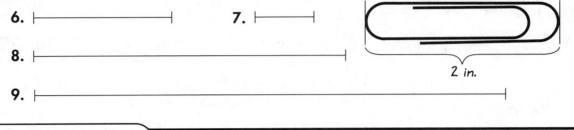

	Estimation Tool	Tool Length	Measurement	Estimated Length
3.	car length	12 ft	3 cars	
4.	shoe length	10 in.	$14\frac{1}{2}$ shoes	
5.	length of baseball bat	1 yd	$\frac{2}{3}$ bat	

Estimate each length. Use the paperclip as an estimation unit.

6. |———————| 7. |———|

2 in.

8. |————————————|

9. |———————————————————|

Application

 It took Betty 134 steps to walk the length of a 100-yard football field.

10. It took her 587 steps to walk from her house to the pizza shop where she works. About how far is that? _____

11. About how many inches long is Betty's stride?

_____

12. Betty goes on a 3-mile walk each day. About how many steps does she take on her walk?_____

COOPERATIVE **13.** Work together to develop measurement units you can use for estimating lengths. How would you estimate each of the following without standard measuring units?

LEARNING

   a. the length and width of an office building _____

   b. the width of a desk _____

   c. the distance to the nearest mall _____

   d. the length of a key _____

CUSTOMARY MEASURE: CAPACITY

Vocabulary

fluid ounce (oz): a customary unit used to measure liquids

cup (c): 8 fluid ounces

pint (pt): 2 cups or 16 fluid ounces

quart (qt): 2 pints or 4 cups or 32 fluid ounces

gallon (gal): 4 quarts or 8 pints or 16 cups or 128 fluid ounces

Reminder

Be sure you write your answer in simplest form.

There are 5 cups of tomato puree in the blender. Mercedes needs 38 ounces of tomato puree for her restaurant's taco sauce. Does she have enough?

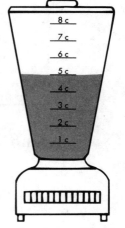

One cup is 8 ounces. Multiply to change a larger unit to a smaller unit.

$$5 \times 8 = 40$$

$$5 \ cups = 40 \ fluid \ ounces$$

Mercedes has enough puree. Mercedes made 54 cups of salsa. How many quart jars can she fill?

Change 54 cups to quarts. 1 quart is 4 cups. Divide to change a smaller unit to a larger unit.

$$54 \div 4 = \frac{54}{4} = 13\frac{2}{4} \ or \ 13\frac{1}{2}$$

$$54 \ cups = 13\frac{1}{2} \ quarts$$

Mercedes can fill 13 quart jars completely.

Guided Practice

Reminder

When multiplying a mixed number, first change it to a fraction.

1. Change $2\frac{1}{2}$ gallons to quarts.

   a. 1 gallon = _____ quarts.

   b. _____ to change a larger unit to a smaller unit.

   c. $4 \times 2\frac{1}{2} =$ _____

   d. $2\frac{1}{2}$ gallons = _____ quarts.

2. Which is more, 24 pints or $2\frac{1}{2}$ gallons?

   a. Change 24 pints to _____

   b. _____ to change a smaller unit to a larger unit.

   c. 24 pints = _____ gallons

   d. _____ is more.

Change each measurement.

3. 2 gal= _____ qt

4. 8 pt = _____ qt

5. $\frac{1}{2}$ pt = _____ c

6. 24 oz = _____ c

7. 1 pt = _____ qt

8. 3 qt = _____ gal

9. 16 c = _____ gal

10. $\frac{1}{4}$ gal = _____ qt

Which is more? Circle your answer.

11. 28 oz or 3 c

12. 12 oz or 1 pt

13. 15 pt or 1 gal

14. 3 oz or $\frac{1}{4}$ c

15. 10 oz or $1\frac{1}{2}$ c

16. 20 oz or 1 qt

17. 12 qt or 4 gal

18. $5\frac{1}{4}$ qt or 20 c

Application

19. Mercedes served 6 quarts of iced tea at her restaurant on Tuesday. One serving of iced tea is 12 ounces. How many 12-ounce servings are in

6 quarts? _____

20. Mr. Li made 15 gallons of chutney. How many 4-ounce bowls can he fill?

_____

21. Joji bought a six-pack of 12-ounce cans of juice. Does he have enough juice to serve 2 cups of juice each to 5 people? If so, will he have any left over? How much? If not, how much more will he need?

_____

22. On a separate sheet of paper, make a display that illustrates the relationship among customary units of liquid measure.

CUSTOMARY MEASURE: WEIGHT

Vocabulary

weight: a measure of the gravitational force exerted on an object. Ounce, pound, and ton are customary units of weight.

ounce (oz): a small customary unit used to measure weight

pound (lb): 16 ounces

ton (T): 2000 pounds

Reminder

Practice estimating at the grocery store. Estimate the weight of fruits or other items, and then weigh them.

Reminder

To "get a feel" for customary units of weight, weigh some objects you lift often, like your shoes or a favorite cup.

Problem 1: Connie Nozaki works at the post office. Letters weighing one ounce or less can be mailed with one stamp. A regular business envelope and three sheets of paper weigh about an ounce. Connie uses this information to determine when just one stamp is required on a letter.

A package weighs 44 ounces. How many pounds is that?

1 pound is 16 ounces.

Divide to change a lighter unit to a heavier unit.

$$44 \div 16 = 2\frac{12}{16}, \text{ or } 2\frac{3}{4}$$

$$44 \text{ ounces} = 2\frac{3}{4} \text{ pound}$$

Problem 2: A city post office processed $3\frac{1}{4}$ tons of mail. How many pounds is that?

1 ton is 2000 pounds.

Multiply to change a heavier unit to a lighter unit.

$$3\frac{1}{4} \times 2000 = \frac{13}{4} \times 2000 = 6500$$

$$3\frac{1}{4} \text{ tons} = 6500 \text{ pounds}$$

Guided Practice

1. Select the best estimate for the weight of a hand-held calculator: 4 ounces, 80 ounces, 4 pounds.

   a. Which choices are too light? _____ *none* _____

   b. Which choices are too heavy? _____

   c. Which choice is the best estimate? _____

2. Change $5\frac{1}{2}$ pounds to ounces.

   a. _____ ounces = 1 pound

   b. _____ to change pounds to ounces.

   c. $5\frac{1}{2} \times 16 =$ _____

   d. $5\frac{1}{2}$ pounds = _____ ounces

Select the best estimate for each weight. Draw a circle around your choice.

3. A bicycle:	24 oz	24 lb	24 T
4. A sports car:	140 lb	1.4 T	14 T
5. A video tape:	9.5 oz	85 oz	.045 lb
6. Two carrots:	0.35 oz	0.35 lb	3.5 lb

Change each measurement.

7. 2.25 lb = _____ oz

8. 1.4 T = _____ lb

9. 64 oz = _____ lb

10. 2600 lb = _____ T

11. 800 lb = _____ T

12. 720 oz = _____ lb

Application

13. A 1.3-ton shipment of chemicals was divided into $\frac{1}{2}$-oz containers. How many containers were needed? _____

14. Improve your estimating sense by sorting and then weighing some things. For example, sort mail by the ounce: 1 ounce or less, 1 to 2 ounces, 2 to 3 ounces, and so on. Or, sort books by the pound.

15. Art knows his weight and the weights of his dog, his bicycle, his jacket, and his toothbrush. How might this knowledge help him estimate the weight of his new baby sister?

_____

_____

16. Discuss situations in which you might want to estimate weight. Which weights do you know that could be used to make estimates?

_____

_____

METRIC MEASURE: LENGTH

Vocabulary

metric system: a base 10 system of measurement. Each unit is larger or smaller than other units by some power of 10.

centimeter (cm): $\frac{1}{100}$ (0.01) meter

1 centimeter

├────┤

meter (m): 10^2 (100) centimeters or $\frac{1}{1000}$ (0.001) kilometer

kilometer (km): 10^3 (1000) meters

Reminder

To multiply by multiples of ten, you can move the decimal point to the right. To divide by multiples of ten, you can move the decimal point to the left.

Problem 1: A city block in Homerville is 75 meters long. It is 2.4 kilometers from Dr. Gorbea's office to the Medical Center. How many blocks is that?

First find how many meters it is from the office to the Medical Center.

$$1 \; kilometer = 1000 \; meters$$

Multiply to change from a longer unit to a shorter unit.

$$2.4 \times 1000 = 2400$$

$$2.4 \; kilometers = 2400 \; meters$$

$$2400 \div 75 = 32$$

It is 32 blocks from the office to the Medical Center.

Problem 2: It is 23 blocks from the Medical Center to the pharmacy. How many kilometers is that? First, find the distance in meters.

$$23 \times 75 = 1775$$

It is 1,775 meters to the pharmacy.

Divide to change a shorter unit to a longer unit.

$$1775 \div 1000 = 1.775$$

It is 1.775 kilometers from the Medical Center to the pharmacy.

Guided Practice

1. Change 3.4 meters to centimeters.

   a. 1 meter = _____ centimeters

   b. _____ to change from a longer unit to a shorter unit.

   c. 3.4 meters = _____ centimeters

2. Write *centimeter, meter* or *kilometer* to complete the statement.

   a. A building is likely to be 200 _____ tall.

b. The length of one's arm is about one _____ long.

c. The length of ten football fields is about one _____.

Exercises

Change each measurement.

3. 50 km = _____ m

4. 690 cm = _____ m

5. 28,900 m = _____ km

6. 17.8 m = _____ cm

7. 0.00462 m = _____ cm

8. 0.009 m = _____ km

Write *cm, m* or *km* to complete each statement.

9. The Empire State Building is 415 _____ tall.

10. A carpenter's hammer is 33 _____ long.

11. Andres drove 15.6 _____ to visit his aunt.

12. A sunflower is 57 _____ tall.

Application

13. In Music City, 14 blocks are about 1 kilometer long. If the blocks are all the same length, about how many meters long is each block?

_____

14. In one month, Julian ran 225 km. How many meters is that?

_____

15. In your opinion, which form presented in the vocabulary section, fraction or decimal, best shows the relationships among the metric units of length? Explain.

_____

_____

_____

16. How many meters long are blocks in your area? Discuss ways to measure the length of a block. Find the lengths of a number of different blocks. Compare your findings with those of other groups.

ESTIMATING LENGTHS IN METRIC UNITS

Problem 1: Ms. Nyborg knits a patch like this on each of her afghans. To plan how much yarn to buy, she estimates its size. What is the approximate length and width of the patch?

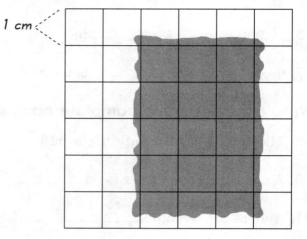

1 cm

The patch is between 3 and $3\frac{1}{2}$ centimeters across, but closer to 3 centimeters. It is about 3 centimeters wide. The patch is a little less than 5 centimeters long, or about 5 centimeters long.

Problem 2: Every section Ms. Nyborg knits is 2.2 centimeters long. If she has knitted 25 sections, about how long is the afghan?

Each section is about 2 centimeters long.

$$25 \times 2 = 50$$

The afghan is about 50 centimeters long, or $\frac{1}{2}$ meter.

Guided Practice

1. Using a 4-centimeter paperclip as an estimating unit, estimate the length of this line.

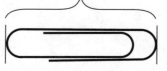

4 centimeters

a. The line is about $2\frac{1}{2}$ times the length of the paperclip.

b. $4 \times 2\frac{1}{2} =$ _____

c. The line is about _____ centimeters long.

2. A poster which is 75 centimeters, or $\frac{3}{4}$ of a meter long, is placed on a wall which is about 4 times its length. How high is the wall?

   a. The poster is _____ meters.

   b. $4 \times \frac{3}{4} =$ _____

   c. The wall is about _____ meters high.

Exercises

Using this measured line as an estimating unit, estimate the length of each line.

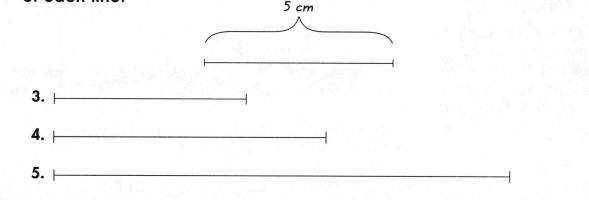

3.

4.

5.

Application

6. The span of Isabel's hand is 18 cm. Her dog is about $3\frac{1}{2}$ spans tall. About how tall is her dog? _____

7. Ved's stride is 75 cm. He walked 564 steps to the store. How many meters away was the store? _____ (Hint: There are 100 cm in a meter.)

COOPERATIVE LEARNING

8. Work together to develop some ways you can estimate length in metric units. How would you estimate each of the following without measuring?

   a. the height of a building _____

   b. the length of a dog's tail _____

   c. the wingspan of a butterfly _____

   d. the distance between your home and the nearest movie theater _____

METRIC MEASURE: CAPACITY

Vocabulary

The following are metric units used to measure liquids.

milliliter (mL): $\frac{1}{10}$ (0.1) centiliter or $\frac{1}{1000}$ (0.001) liter

centiliter (cL): 10^1 (10) milliliters or $\frac{1}{100}$ (0.01) liter

liter (L): 10^3 (1000) milliliters or 10^2 (100) centiliters

Reminder

Move the decimal point to the right to multiply by multiples of 10. Move the decimal point to the left to divide by multiples of 10.

Problem 1: Naomi works at a juice bar. She squeezed 160 milliliters of juice from one grapefruit. How many grapefruits will she need to make enough juice to fill a 2-liter pitcher?

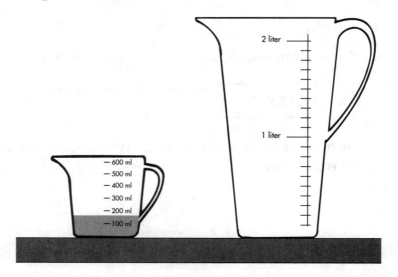

1 liter is 1000 milliliters. Multiply to change from a larger unit to a smaller unit.

$$2 \text{ liters} = 2 \times 1000, \text{ or } 2000 \text{ milliliters}$$
$$2000 \div 160 = 12.5$$

Naomi will need 13 grapefruits, since the juice from 12 grapefruits is not enough to fill the 2-liter pitcher.

Problem 2: A 25-centiliter glass of grapefruit juice sells for $1.50. How many 25-centiliter glasses can be filled from a 2-liter pitcher? How much money will be made?

$$10 \text{ milliliters} = 1 \text{ centiliter}$$

Divide to change from a smaller unit to a larger unit.

$$2000 \text{ milliliters} \div 10 = 200 \text{ centiliters}$$
$$200 \div 25 = 8, \text{ or } 8 \text{ 25-centiliter glasses of juice}$$
$$8 \times \$1.50 = \$12.00$$

A 2-liter pitcher will make $12.00.

1. If a new cold medicine costs $5.00 for each milliliter, how much will 10 centiliters cost?

   a. 1 centiliter = _____10_____ milliliters

   b. _____ to change centiliters to milliliters.

   c. Move the decimal to the right: 10 centiliters = _____ milliliters.

   d. $5.00 × 100 milliliters = _____

   e. 10 centiliters costs _____

Exercises

Select the best unit of metric liquid measure for each container.

2. a bathtub _____   3. a soup bowl _____

4. an eye dropper _____   5. a baby bottle _____

Change each unit of measure.

6. 200 mL = _____ cL   7. 500 cL = _____ L

8. 1200 mL = _____ L   9. 36.2 L = _____ cL

10. 44.4 cL = _____ mL   11. 7.1 L = _____ mL

Application

12. How many 500-mL glasses of juice can Naomi pour from a 5-liter pitcher? If each glass is $1.25, how much will 5 liters cost?

    _____

13. One day Naomi sold 16 of the 250-mL glasses of juice for 75 cents each, and 22 of the 500-mL glasses of juice at $1.25 each. How many liters of juice did she have to make? How much money did she make?

    _____

14. Make a display that illustrates the relationship among milliliter, centiliter, and liter units.

METRIC MEASURE: MASS

Vocabulary

mass: the measure of the amount of matter in an object. Mass can be measured with a balance scale.

milligram (mg): $\frac{1}{1000}$ (0.001) gram

gram (g): 10^3 (1000) milligrams or $\frac{1}{1000}$ (0.001) kilogram

kilogram (kg): 10^3 (1000) grams

Reminder

To improve your "feel" for metric units of mass, notice the mass of objects you are familiar with. For example: A cat is about 2 kilograms. A baseball is about 145 grams. An aspirin tablet is about 200 milligrams.

Problem 1: A large egg is 50 grams. How many kilograms is that?

1 kilogram is 1000 grams.

Divide to change from a smaller unit to a larger unit.

$$50 \div 1000 = 0.050$$

Move the decimal point 3 places to the left.

50 grams = 0.05 kilograms

Problem 2: How many milligrams is a 50-gram egg?

Multiply to change from a larger unit to a smaller unit.

$$50 \times 1000 = 50.000$$

Move the decimal point 3 places to the right.

50 grams = 50,000 milligrams

Nutrition Facts
1 Grade A Large Egg (50g)
Calories: 70
Total fat: 4.5g
Cholesterol: 215 mg
Carbohydrates: 1 g
Protein: 6 g
Sodium: 65 mg

Guided Practice

1. Is the mass of an apple closest to

    200 milligrams   200 grams   200 kilograms

    a. Which choices are too small? _____

    b. Which choices are too large? _____

    c. Which is the best choice? _____

2. Change 6.25 kilograms to grams.

    a. 1 kilogram = _____ grams

    b. To change kilograms to grams, _____.

    c. 6.25 kilograms = _____ grams

Exercises

Which is the best estimate of the mass? Circle your answer.

3. A pair of basketball shoes   1000 mg   11.1 g   1.1 kg

4. A dose of medicine   0.55 mg   5.5 g   0.5 kg

5. Sodium in 12 potato chips   125 mg   125 g   1.25 kg

6. An elephant   4500 g   450 kg   4500 kg

Change each measurement.

7. 8.3 mg = _____ g

8. 7500 g = _____ kg

9. 0.057 g = _____ mg

10. 0.54 kg = _____ g

11. 7,002,000 mg = _____ kg

12. 0.0019 g = _____ mg

Application

13. A basket has a mass of 60 g. When filled with eggs, it has a mass of 1.4 kg. Assume the basket contains large eggs with a mass of about 50 g each. How many eggs would you expect to be in the basket?

_____

14. 6 eggs have a mass of 330 g. What is the average mass of an egg?

_____

15. Brian buys 2 kg of ground meat to make hamburgers for his friends. If each hamburger is 125 g, how many hamburgers can Brian make?

_____

16. How small is a milligram? Use a scientific scale and create a display showing the mass of items such as salt, seeds, flower petals, and dust.

LINES, RAYS, AND LINE SEGMENTS

Vocabulary

point: one exact location, as where two lines meet

•
point

line: a set of points that extend without end in either direction

⟵————————⟶
line

ray: part of a line that extends in one direction and has one endpoint

•————————⟶
ray

line segment: part of a line with two endpoints

•————————•
line segment

parallel lines: lines in the same plane that do not meet

⟵————————⟶
⟵————————⟶
parallel lines

perpendicular lines: lines that meet forming equal angles

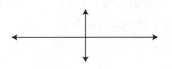
perpendicular lines

Reminder

In everyday speech "line," rather than "line segment," is sometimes used. Parallel line segments are called parallel lines; perpendicular line segments are called perpendicular lines.

Which types of lines did LaKeisha use to make a line drawing of this light house?

She used: Parallel lines for the sides of the lighthouse

Perpendicular lines for windows

Rays to show the directions of light

Line segments to connect elements of the drawing

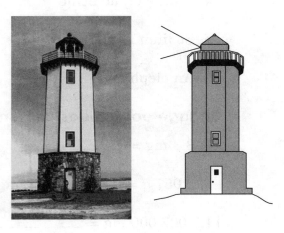

Guided Practice

Match each term with its drawing.

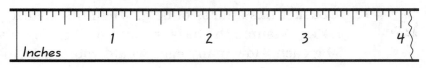

1. parallel lines

  a. Which lines do not meet? _____

  b. The part of the drawing that shows parallel lines is _____

2. perpendicular lines

  a. Which lines meet and form equal angles?

  _____

  b. The part of the drawing that shows perpendicular lines is _____

Exercises

Match the term with its illustration.

3. line   **a.**

4. ray(s)   **b.**

5. line segment(s)   **c.**

6. parallel lines   **d.**

7. perpendicular lines   **e.**

8. point(s)   **f.**

Application

9. Artists use perspective in their drawings. These drawings show shapes that have perpendicular lines. Why are the lines not actually perpendicular on flat paper?

_____

_____

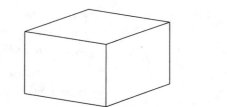 

10. Select a structure, such as a milk carton, a desk or a building. Identify and describe parallel and perpendicular line segments in the structure.

_____

_____

_____

11. Sketch your structure. Challenge a classmate to find examples of the types of lines discussed in this lesson.

12. Use different colors to identify the parallel and perpendicular line segments in this drawing.

ANGLES AND ANGLE MEASURE

Vocabulary

angle: two rays with the same endpoint

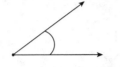

degree: the unit used to measure angles. A degree is $\frac{1}{360}$ of a circle and written with the symbol °.

An angle measuring 1°

protractor: a tool marked in degrees and used to measure angles

A Protractor

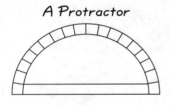

straight angle: an angle in which the two rays form a line

Reminder

To make accurate measurements, check that one side of the angle is on the zero line.

A protractor has two scales. Which scale should you use to find an angle measure?

Place the endpoint of the angle on the protractor's center point. Align one side of the angle on the zero line.

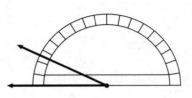

The side of the angle above is on the zero mark for the outside scale. Read the outside scale to find the angle measure. This angle measures 25°.

The side of the angle to the right is on the zero mark for the inside scale. Read the inside scale to find the angle measure. This angle measures 140°.

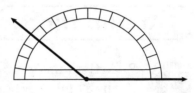

Angles can be classified by their measure.

An angle whose rays are perpendicular and which measures 90° is a right angle

An angle measuring less than a right angle is an acute angle

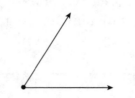

An angle measuring greater than a right angle is an obtuse angle

Guided Practice

1. Measure and classify each angle.

    a. Use a protractor to measure the three angles in this triangle.

    b. Decide whether each angle measures 90°, less than 90°, or more than 90°.

Exercises

Measure and classify each numbered angle in the figure.

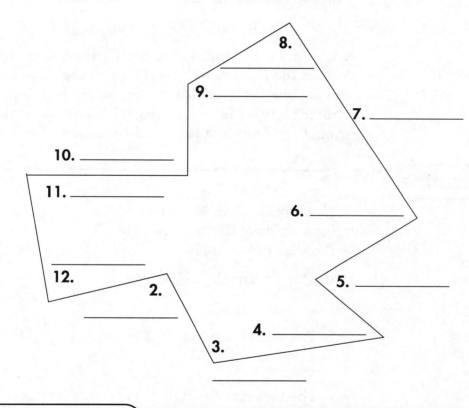

Application

13. Work together to complete the chart. Find examples of various angles in your environment and experience.

Angle Classification	Angle Measure	Examples
Right Angle		
	Less than 90°	
Obtuse Angle		
	180°	

SUM OF THE ANGLES OF A TRIANGLE

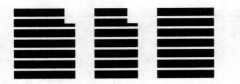

Reminder

You can name an angle with a capital letter that stands for the angle's endpoint.

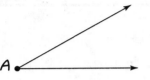

Roberto is making a mosaic using copies of a 35°, 45°, 100° triangle. So far, his mosaic looks like this. What is the sum of the angles in each triangle?

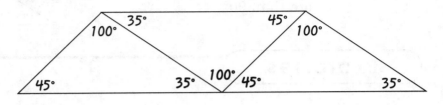

Add the measurements of the three angles.

$$35 + 45 + 100 = 180$$

The sum of the angles of Roberto's triangle is 180°. Now look at the point where the three triangles meet. You can see the three angles side by side. They form a straight angle that measures 180°. This shows that the sum of the angles of Roberto's triangle is 180°.

Guided Practice

1. Use a protractor. Measure each angle of the triangle. Find the sum of the angles.

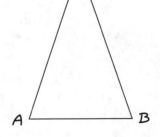

   a. The measure of angle A is

   _____72_____°.

   b. The measure of angle B is

   _____°.

   c. The measure of angle C is

   _____°.

   d. The sum of the angles is

   ____72____ + _____ + _____ = _____

Use a protractor. Measure each angle of the triangle. Find the sum of the angles.

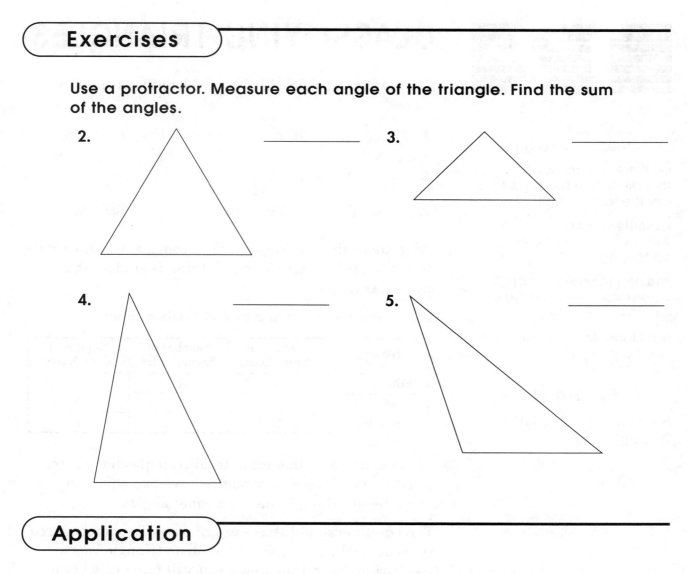

2. _____

3. _____

4. _____

5. _____

Application

6. Work in groups of four. Have each member cut out a triangle like one of the four in the Exercises. Fold each triangle as shown.

Step 1   Step 2   Step 3

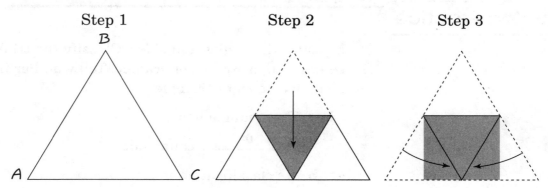

Look at angles A, B, and C in Step 1 of the model. Where are these same angles in Step 3? What does the model show about the relationship among the angles of a triangle?

_____

_____

CLASSIFYING TRIANGLES

Triangles can be classified by the lengths of their sides.

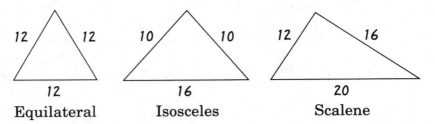

Equilateral   Isosceles   Scalene

Vocabulary

equilateral triangle: a triangle with three sides that are the same length

isosceles triangle: a triangle with two sides that are the same length

scalene triangle: a triangle whose sides are all different lengths

right triangle: a triangle with one right angle

Reminder

An angle that measures 90° is a right angle.

From these three examples, what conclusions can Tonya draw about the *angles* of equilateral, isosceles, and scalene triangles?

Tonya measured the angles and made a table:

Triangle	Number of Equal Sides	Number of Equal Angles	Number of Right Angles
Equilateral	3	3	0
Isosceles	2	2	0
Scalene	0	0	1

Tonya concluded that equilateral triangles have three equal angles, isosceles triangles have two equal angles, and scalene triangles have no equal angles.

The equilateral and isosceles triangles Tonya measured were not right triangles. The scalene triangle was a right triangle. In this lesson you will find out whether what Tonya found is true in all cases.

Guided Practice

Measure the angles and sides. Classify the triangle as equilateral, isosceles, or scalene. Tell whether the triangle is a right triangle.

1. a. The triangle has

_____0_____ equal sides

b. Its classification is _____

c. The angle measures are:
_98°, 25°, 57°_

d. The triangle has _____ equal angles.

e. Is the triangle a right triangle? _____

2. a. The triangle has _____ equal sides

b. Its classification is _____ .

c. The angle measures are _____ .

d. The triangle has _____ equal angles.

e. Is the triangle a right triangle? _____

Exercises

Use a ruler and a protractor. Classify each triangle as equilateral, isosceles, or scalene. Then find the number of equal angles and the number of right angles. Complete the table.

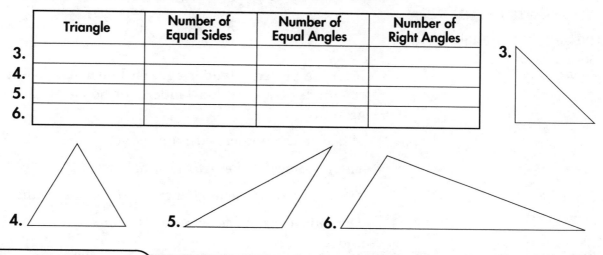

	Triangle	Number of Equal Sides	Number of Equal Angles	Number of Right Angles
3.				
4.				
5.				
6.				

3.

4. **5.** **6.**

Application

Can each type of triangle be a right triangle? If so, draw an example. If not, explain why not.

7. An equilateral triangle   **8.** An isosceles triangle   **9.** A scalene triangle

_____   _____   _____

_____   _____   _____

10. Write a procedure (a sequence of steps) you could use to classify triangles.

_____

_____

_____

MEASURE OF AN EXTERIOR ANGLE OF A TRIANGLE

Vocabulary

interior angle: an angle inside of a triangle

exterior angle: an angle formed by extending one side of a triangle

remote interior angles: the two interior angles that are not next to the exterior angle

Reminder

The sum of the angle measures of a triangle is 180°.

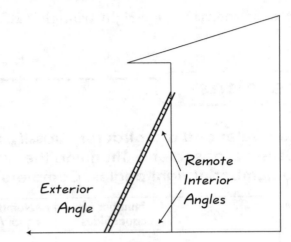

Radhika placed a ladder against her house. What are the angles between her ladder, her house, and the ground?

Measure the angles with a protractor.

The measure of the exterior angle is 115°.

The measure of the angle next to the exterior angle is 65°.

The measures of the remote interior angles are 90° and 25°.

Guided Practice

Using a protractor, find the measure of the exterior angle and of each of the interior angles.

1. **a.** Measure the exterior angle. _____

   b. Measure the angle next to the exterior angle. _____ °

   c. Which angles are the remote interior angles? _____ *The two angles that are not next to the exterior angle.*

   d. The measures of the remote interior angles are _____ ° and _____ °.

Use a protractor to complete the table. For each triangle, find the measure of the exterior angle and of each interior angle.

	Measurements		
	Exterior Angle	**Angle Next to Exterior Angle**	**Remote Interior Angles**
2.			
3.			
4.			

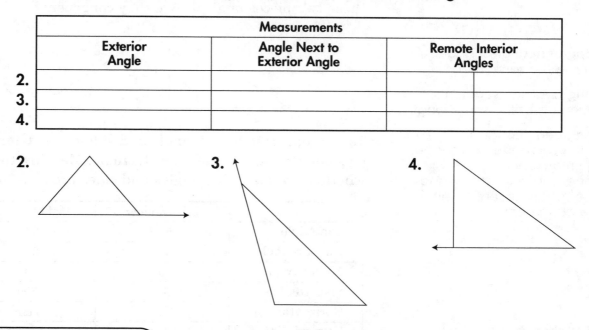

Application

5. Use the table you created in the Exercises. What is the relationship between the exterior angle of a triangle and the two remote interior angles?

6. If you know the measure of an exterior angle, how can you find the measure of the interior angle that is next to it?

7. The sum of the measures of the angles of a triangle is 180°. How does this fact help explain your answers to questions 5 and 6?

CONGRUENT TRIANGLES

Vocabulary

congruent angles: angles having the same measure

congruent line segments: line segments of the same length

congruent triangles: triangles of the same size and shape. The matching, or corresponding, angles and sides of congruent triangles are congruent

Abu wants the two triangular windows in his greenhouse to be the same size and shape. He cut these two pieces of glass. Are they congruent?

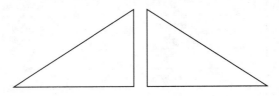

To find out, match each angle and side of one triangle to one side or angle of the other triangle. Measure to check whether the matching angles and sides are congruent.

	Left Window	Right Window
Top Angle	57°	57°
Outside Angle	33°	33°
Middle Angle	90°	90°
Slanted Side	3.6 cm	3.6 cm
Horizontal Side	3 cm	3 cm
Vertical Side	2 cm	2 cm

Matching, or corresponding, angle measures and side lengths are congruent, so the two pieces of glass are congruent.

Guided Practice

Reminder

A figure that is the same size and shape as another figure will fit exactly on top of it. You can trace or cut out triangles to test for congruence.

1. Are these triangles congruent?
   a. Measure the sides of the top triangle. _1.5 cm, 3 cm, 2.3 cm_

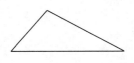

   b. Measure the sides of the bottom triangle. _1.8 cm, 3 cm, 2.6 cm_

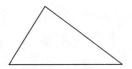

   c. Measure the angles of the top triangle.
      _108°, 26°, 46°_

   d. Measure the angles of the bottom triangle.
      _87°, 37°, 56°_

   e. The triangles have _____ congruent angle(s).

   f. The triangles have _____ congruent side(s).

   g. Are the triangles congruent? _____

Exercises

Are the two triangles congruent?

2.

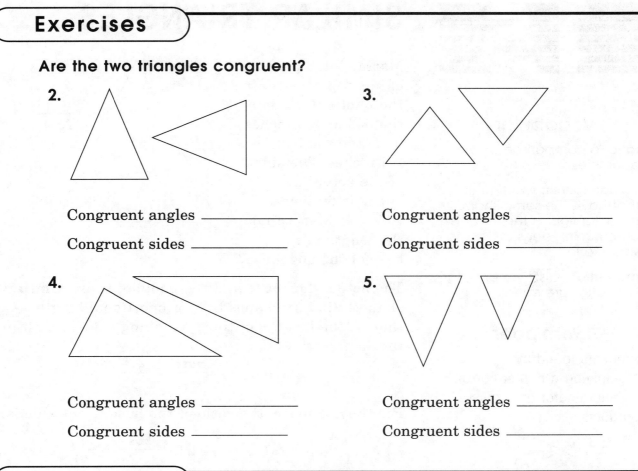

Congruent angles _____

Congruent sides _____

3.

Congruent angles _____

Congruent sides _____

4.

Congruent angles _____

Congruent sides _____

5.

Congruent angles _____

Congruent sides _____

Application

6. Draw and cut out a triangle. Measure the sides and angles of your triangle. Then draw as many *different* looking triangles as you can that have those same sides and angles.

7. From the activity above, what would you conclude about the number of different triangles you can make from three particular side lengths and three particular angles?

_____

_____

8. Compare your triangles from Exercise 6 and your conclusions from Exercise 7 with those of other members of your group. What conclusions hold true for all of your triangles?

_____

_____

SIMILAR TRIANGLES

Vocabulary

ratio: a comparison of two quantities

similar figures: two figures that have the same shape. In similar figures the lengths of matching sides are in the same ratio.

proportion: a statement that two ratios are equal

Reminder

Products found by multiplying a numerator and a denominator are cross-products.

Maria took a photo of her dog's house. In the photo, the side of the house is 3 inches long and the base is 2.5 inches. The side of the actual dog-house is 60 inches. How can Maria find the length of the base of the doghouse?

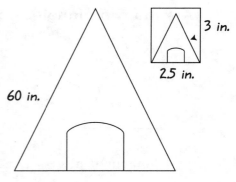

The actual doghouse and the photo of it are **similar** shapes. Similar shapes have proportional lengths—that is, the lengths of their matching sides are all in the same ratio.

$$Photo: \frac{base}{side} = \frac{2.5}{3}$$

For the doghouse, the ratio of the base to the side is:

$$Actual\ dog\ house: \frac{base}{side} = \frac{?}{60}$$

You can solve a proportion to find the missing length—the base of the actual doghouse.

$$\frac{2.5}{3} = \frac{actual\ base}{60}$$

$2.5 \times 60 = 3 \times actual\ base$ Find the cross products.

$150 = 3 \times actual\ base$ Multiply 2.5×60.

$\dfrac{150}{3} = \dfrac{3 \times actual\ base}{3}$ Divide both sides by 3.

$50 = actual\ base$

The base of the doghouse is 50 inches long.

Guided Practice

1. Are the two triangles similar?

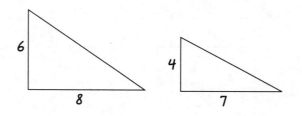

a. Write ratios for the height and width of each triangle.

$$\frac{\text{height}}{\text{width}} = \frac{6}{8}, \frac{\text{height}}{\text{width}} = \frac{4}{7}$$

b. Use cross products to decide if the ratios are equal.

$$\frac{6}{8} ? \frac{4}{7} \qquad 6 \times 7 ? 8 \times 4 \qquad 42 \neq 32$$

c. If the triangles are similar, the two ratios will be equal. Are the triangles similar? _____

Exercises

Show whether each pair of triangles is similar. Write a proportion to test for equal ratios.

2.

3.

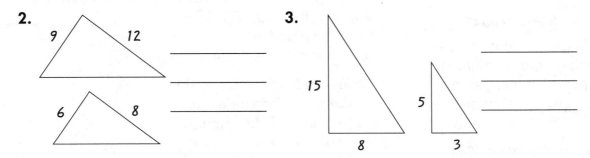

_____

_____

_____

The two triangles are similar. Find the length of side _m_.

4.

5.

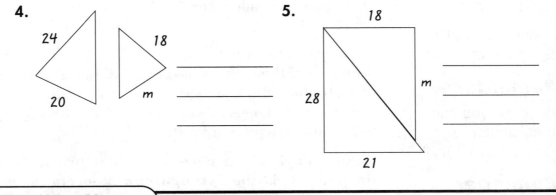

_____

_____

_____

Application

6. George is 72 inches tall. One day his shadow was 18 inches long at the same time that the shadow of a flagpole was 120 inches long. How tall is the flag pole?

_____

_____

RIGHT TRIANGLES AND THE PYTHAGOREAN THEOREM

Chidori found this drawing. What does the drawing explain about the Pythagorean theorem? Chidori asked some friends.

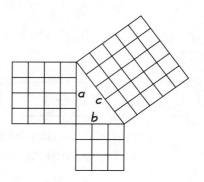

Illustration of the Pythagorean Theorem

Nick said: The triangle is a **right triangle**. The sides are labeled, a, b, and c. Side a is 4 units long, side b is 3 units long and side c is 5 units long. $a = 4$, $b = 3$, $c = 5$

Jenny said: The sides of the squares are the same lengths as the sides of the triangle. The square on side a has 4×4, or 16 units. The square on side b has 3×3, or 9 units. The square on side c has 5×5, or 25 units.

$$4 \times 4 = 16$$
$$3 \times 3 = 9$$
$$5 \times 5 = 25$$

Nick said: I see a pattern. The sum of the squares of the two shorter sides equals the square of the longest side. You can write an equation for it.

$$16 + 9 = 25$$
$$\text{OR}$$
$$4^2 + 3^2 = 5^2$$

Jenny said: I bet the same is true for all right triangles. In other words, the **Pythagorean theorem** can be written $a^2 + b^2 = c^2$.

To test Jenny's conclusion, Chidori drew a right triangle with sides 10 in. and 24 in. If Jenny's conclusion was right, then:

$$10^2 + 24^2 = c^2$$
$$100 + 576 = c^2$$
$$676 = c^2$$

The square root of 676 = c
$$26 = c$$

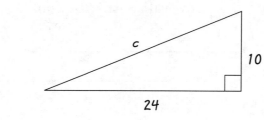

Chidori checked by measuring. $c = 26$

Jenny said: $a^2 + b^2 = c^2$ holds for this right triangle. Let's see if it works for some other right triangles.

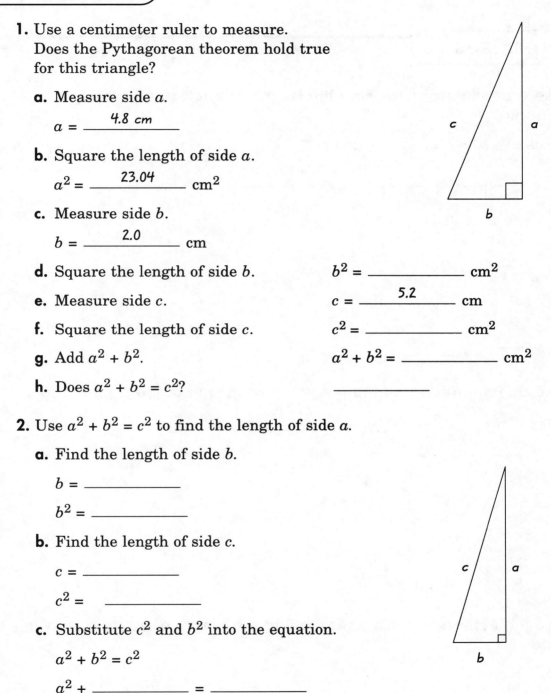

Guided Practice

1. Use a centimeter ruler to measure. Does the Pythagorean theorem hold true for this triangle?

   a. Measure side a.

   $a = $ ___4.8 cm___

   b. Square the length of side a.

   $a^2 = $ ___23.04___ cm^2

   c. Measure side b.

   $b = $ ___2.0___ cm

   d. Square the length of side b. $b^2 = $ _____ cm^2

   e. Measure side c. $c = $ ___5.2___ cm

   f. Square the length of side c. $c^2 = $ _____ cm^2

   g. Add $a^2 + b^2$. $a^2 + b^2 = $ _____ cm^2

   h. Does $a^2 + b^2 = c^2$? _____

2. Use $a^2 + b^2 = c^2$ to find the length of side a.

   a. Find the length of side b.

   $b = $ _____

   $b^2 = $ _____

   b. Find the length of side c.

   $c = $ _____

   $c^2 = $ _____

   c. Substitute c^2 and b^2 into the equation.

   $a^2 + b^2 = c^2$

   $a^2 + $ _____ $= $ _____

   d. Subtract b^2 from both sides of the equation.

   $a^2 = $ _____ $-$ _____

e. Find the difference.

$a^2 = $ _____

f. Find the square root of both sides of the equation.

$a = $ _____

Exercises

Use a centimeter ruler. Find the length of each side of the right triangle.

Does $a^2 + b^2 = c^2$?

3.

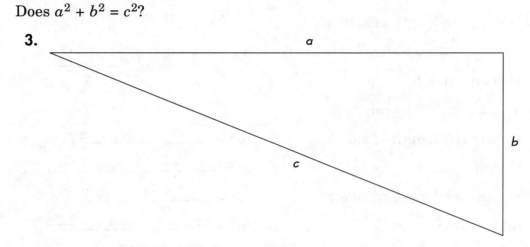

Use an inch ruler. Find the length of each side of the right triangle.

Does $a^2 + b^2 = c^2$?

4.

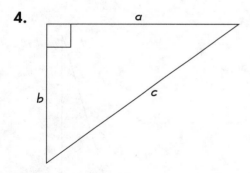

Use the Pythagorean theorem to find the length of each unknown side.

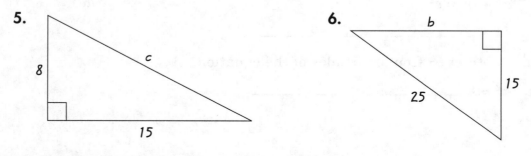

5.

6.

7.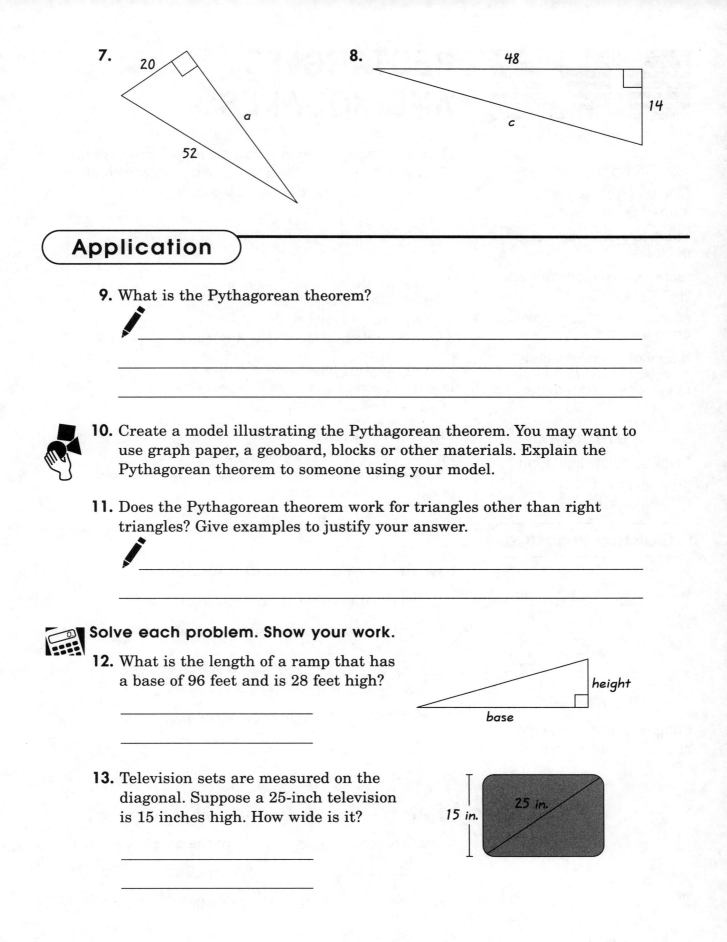
20

52

a

8.
48

c

14

Application

9. What is the Pythagorean theorem?

✏️ _____

_____

_____

10. Create a model illustrating the Pythagorean theorem. You may want to use graph paper, a geoboard, blocks or other materials. Explain the Pythagorean theorem to someone using your model.

11. Does the Pythagorean theorem work for triangles other than right triangles? Give examples to justify your answer.

✏️ _____

_____

Solve each problem. Show your work.

12. What is the length of a ramp that has a base of 96 feet and is 28 feet high?

_____

_____

height

base

13. Television sets are measured on the diagonal. Suppose a 25-inch television is 15 inches high. How wide is it?

_____

_____

15 in.

25 in.

RECTANGLES AND SQUARES

Vocabulary

polygon: a closed figure formed by line segments

quadrilateral: a four-sided polygon

rectangle: a quadrilateral with four right angles

square: a rectangle with four congruent sides

diagonal: a line segment that joins two vertices, or points where sides meet, of a polygon

Reminder

Perpendicular lines form right angles. A right angle measures 90°.

How are a square and a rectangle alike? How are they different? To explore these questions, you can compare the angles, side lengths, and diagonals.

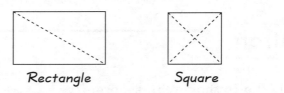

Rectangle   Square   Diagonal

The square has four right angles.
The rectangle has four right angles.

The square has four sides of equal length. The rectangle has two pairs of sides of equal length.

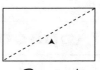

The square has diagonals that are perpendicular and of equal length.
The rectangle has diagonals that are not perpendicular, but are of equal length.

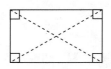

Guided Practice

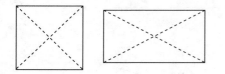

Reminder

Congruent line segments have the same length.

Use a ruler and a protractor to compare.

1. Are the diagonals congruent?

   a. Measure the diagonals of the square.

   _____

   b. Are they congruent? _____

   c. Measure the diagonals of the rectangle.

   _____

   d. Are they congruent? _____

2. Are the diagonals perpendicular to each other?

   a. Measure the angles where the diagonals meet.

     Square_____ Rectangle _____

   b. For which shape are the diagonals perpendicular?

   _____

3. Do the two diagonals form right triangles? _____

    a. Measure the triangles formed by the crossing diagonals.

    b. In which shape do the diagonals form right triangles? _____

Exercises

Use a ruler and a protractor to compare squares and rectangles.

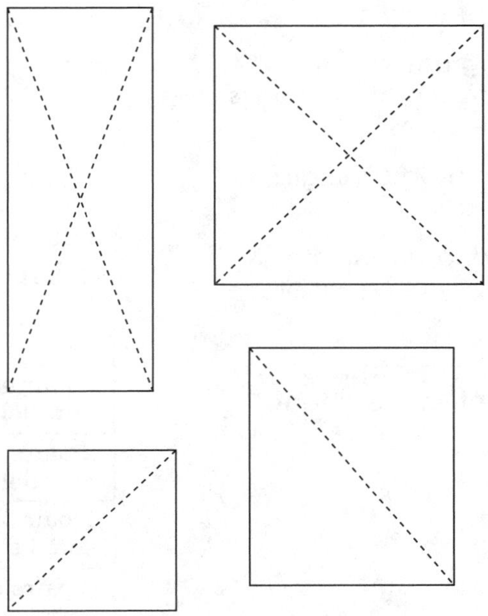

4. Are all side lengths congruent?

    Square _____

    Rectangle _____

5. Are the diagonals congruent?

    Square _____

    Rectangle _____

6. Are the triangles formed by one diagonal right triangles?

    Square _____

    Rectangle _____

7. Are the triangles formed by two diagonals isosceles?

    Square _____ Rectangle _____

8. Are the triangles formed by one diagonal congruent?

    Square _____ Rectangle _____

9. Do the diagonals divide each other into two congruent segments?

    Square _____ Rectangle _____

Application

COOPERATIVE
LEARNING

10. Work together. How are squares and rectangles alike ?

_____

_____

CLASSIFYING QUADRILATERALS

Vocabulary

kite: a quadrilateral with two pairs of congruent sides, but opposite sides are not congruent

parallelogram: a quadrilateral with two pairs of parallel sides

rhombus: a parallelogram with four congruent sides

trapezoid: a quadrilateral with exactly one pair of parallel sides

bisect: to cut into two congruent line segments

How can you compare different kinds of quadrilaterals?

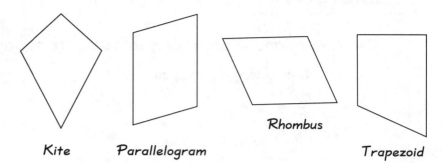

Kite   Parallelogram   Rhombus   Trapezoid

Michelle looked at the properties of sides to compare the quadrilaterals above:

	Kite	Parallelogram	Rhombus	Trapezoid
1 pair of parallel sides		✓	✓	✓
2 pairs of parallel sides		✓	✓	
1 pair of equal sides	✓	✓	✓	
2 pairs of equal sides	✓	✓	✓	
adjacent sides are congruent	✓		✓	
opposite sides are congruent		✓	✓	

Guided Practice

1. You can also explore diagonals to compare quadrilaterals. Use a ruler and a protractor to complete the table.

   a. Measure the length of the diagonals of each quadrilateral.

   b. Measure whether the diagonals cut each other into equal segments.

   c. Measure the angles at which the diagonals intersect.

   d. Measure whether the angles on each side of the diagonals have the same measure.

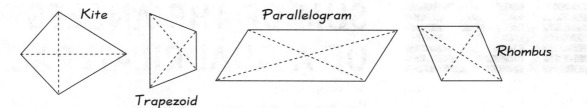

Kite   Parallelogram

Trapezoid   Rhombus

	Kite	Trapezoid	Rhombus	Parallelogram
diagonals are congruent				
diagonals bisect each other				
diagonals are perpendicular				
diagonals bisect the angles				

Exercises

You can compare angles to compare quadrilaterals. Use a protractor to complete the table.

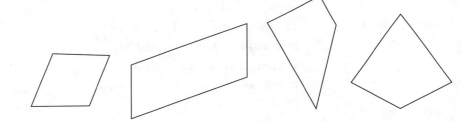

		Rhombus	Parallelogram	Trapezoid	Kite
2.	opposite angles are equal				
3.	adjacent angles are equal				
4.	opposite angles have a sum of 180°				
5.	adjacent angles have a sum of 180°				

Application

Decide if the statement is true or false. Explain your thinking.

6. If a quadrilateral has four congruent sides, its diagonals bisect.

_____

_____

SUM OF THE ANGLES OF A QUADRILATERAL

Reminder

For any triangle, the sum of the angle measures is 180°.

Reminder

Opposite angles of a rhombus have the same measure.

You can discover more about quadrilaterals by investigating the sum of their angle measures. What is the sum of the angles of a square?

Lu figures this way:
The four angles of a square are right angles. The measure of a right angle is 90°. The sum of the angles of a square is 4 × 90°, or 360°.

Bella reasons:
A diagonal cuts a square into two triangles. The sum of the angles of a triangle is 180°. The sum of the angles of two triangles that make a square is 2 × 180°, or 360°.

Guided Practice

1. Measure the angles of the rhombus. Then find the sum of the measures. Use a protractor if you need to .

   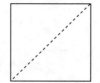

   a. Angle A: _____   **b.** Angle C: _____

   c. Angle B: _____   **d.** Angle D: _____

   e. The sum of the angle measures is _____.

2. Draw a diagonal to help you find the sum of the angles of the trapezoid.

   a. How many triangles are formed? _____

   b. The sum of the measures of the angles of each triangle is _____.

   c. The sum of the angles of the trapezoid is _____.

Exercises

Name the quadrilateral and find the sum of its angle measures. You may want to use a protractor.

3.

Name: _____

Sum: _____

4.

Name: _____

Sum: _____

5.

Name: _____

Sum: _____

6.

Name: _____

Sum: _____

Application

7. What conclusions can you draw about the sum of the angle measures of a quadrilateral? Can you find any exceptions? If so, draw the exception.

_____

_____

8. Lucy drew both diagonals of the rectangle. She concluded that the sum of the angles of the rectangle is 4 × 180° = 720°. Is she correct? Why or why not? (Hint: A rectangle always has only 4 angles)

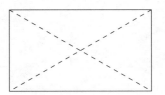

_____

_____

PERIMETER

In Messenger Park, a basketball court is marked off on the blacktop. It is a rectangle 85 feet long and 46 feet wide. What ways are there to find the perimeter of the court?

Vocabulary

perimeter: the distance around a polygon

regular polygon: a polygon whose sides and angles are all of equal measure

Reminder

A rectangle has two pairs of sides of equal length.

Reminder

Multiply before you add.

John says: Find the sum of the side lengths.
P = length + width + length + width
P = 85 + 46 + 85 + 46 = 262
The perimeter of the basketball court is 262 feet.

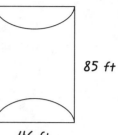

85 ft

46 ft

Doreen says:
Find the sum of 2 lengths and 2 widths.
P = 2 × length + 2 × width
P = 2 × 85 + 2 × 46
P = 170 + 92 = 262
The perimeter of the basketball court is 262 feet.

Both methods work to find the distance around the court.

Guided Practice

Reminder

To estimate with mixed numbers or decimals, you can round to a near whole number.

1. Find the perimeter of the polygon.

$4\frac{1}{2}$ m

$1\frac{1}{4}$ m   2 m

$5\frac{3}{4}$ m

a. P = _____ + _____ + _____ + _____

b. P = _____ m

c. Estimate to check the answer. The perimeter is
about ___1___ + ___5___ + ___2___ + ___6___ = _____ m

d. Is the answer reasonable? _____

2. Find the perimeter of a regular hexagon, or six-sided polygon, with sides each measuring 2.5 cm. Write a formula for the perimeter of a regular hexagon.

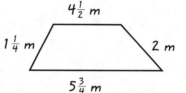

2.5 cm

a. Number of sides: _____6_____ **b.** Side length: _____ cm

c. P = _____ × _____ **d.** P = _____

e. Let *s* be the length of one side of a regular hexagon.

A formula for finding the perimeter of a regular hexagon is P = _____ *s*.

Exercises

Find the perimeter of each polygon. Estimate to check your answer.

3.

$21\frac{1}{3}$ ft
10 ft
$8\frac{5}{6}$ ft
$14\frac{2}{3}$ ft

Perimeter _____

Estimate _____

4.

Kite

5.2 m   7.8 m

Perimeter _____

Estimate _____

5.

18.9 cm   17.7 cm   45.9 cm
20.2 cm   71.4 cm

Perimeter _____

Estimate _____

Find the perimeter of each regular polygon. Then write a formula for finding the perimeter. Let *s* be the side of the regular polygon.

6.

6.8 m

Perimeter _____

Formula _____

7.

$5\frac{1}{4}$ ft

Perimeter _____

Formula _____

8.

$16\frac{5}{8}$ in.

Perimeter _____

Formula _____

Application

9. What generalization can you make about the formula for finding the perimeter of any regular polygon?

_____

_____

10. Alexander used 740 feet of fencing around his rectangular garden. The garden is 214.5 feet long. How wide is it? _____

AREA OF SQUARES AND RECTANGLES

Vocabulary

area: the number of square units needed to cover a region

Reminder

To square a number or unit, multiply the number or unit by itself. A square measuring 1 unit in length by 1 unit in length is 1 square unit in area. Square units can be written: (unit)^2. For example, yd^2, cm^2, or ft^2.

Problem 1: A playground is paved in concrete sections that are 1 yard square. What is the area of the playground?

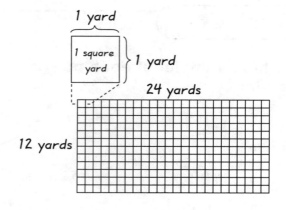

The area can be found by multiplying length by width.

A (area) = length $\times$ width, or A = lw

$l = 24$, $w = 12$ A = 24 $\times$ 12

A = 288 square yards

The area of the playground is 288 yd^2.

Problem 2: What is the area of each section of concrete in square feet?

A yard is 3 feet. Each section of concrete has 3-foot sides. The area can be found by multiplying length by width, which for a square are the same length.

A (area) = side $\times$ side, or A = s^2

A = 3 $\times$ 3

A = 9 square feet

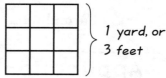

The area of each section of concrete is 9 ft^2.

Guided Practice

Reminder

Tick marks can be used to show line segments of equal length. This figure is a rectangle, having opposite sides of equal length.

Use the formulas A = lw and A = s^2.

1. Find the area.

    a. The figure is a _____ .

    b. Use the formula _____ .

25.6 m

c. The sides are _____ m long.

d. The area is _____ square meters, or m².

2. Find the width of this rectangle.

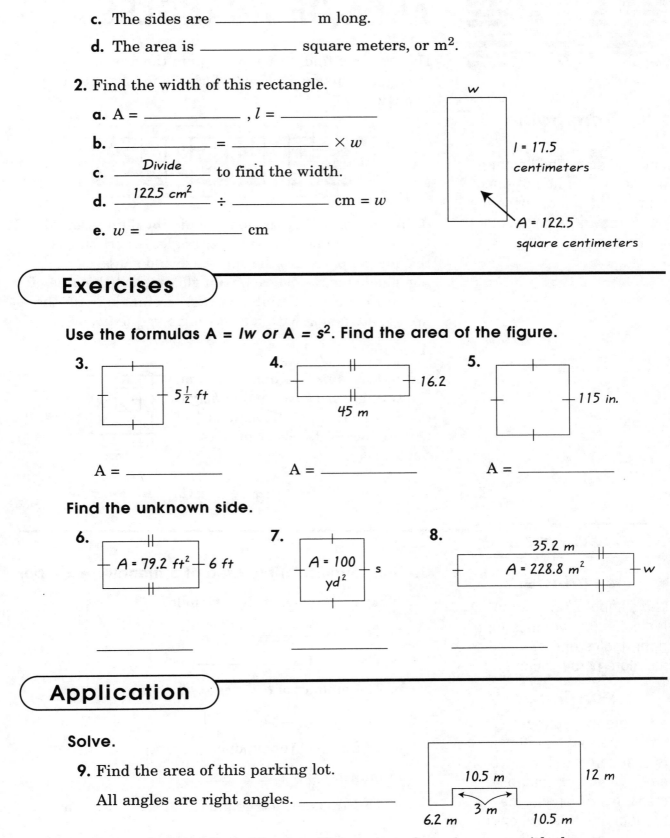

a. A = _____ , l = _____

b. _____ = _____ × w

c. _____Divide_____ to find the width.

d. _____122.5 cm²_____ ÷ _____ cm = w

e. w = _____ cm

l = 17.5 centimeters

A = 122.5 square centimeters

Exercises

Use the formulas A = lw or A = s^2. Find the area of the figure.

3. $5\frac{1}{2}$ ft

A = _____

4. 16.2

45 m

A = _____

5. 115 in.

A = _____

Find the unknown side.

6. A = 79.2 ft²   6 ft

_____

7. A = 100 yd²   s

_____

8. 35.2 m   A = 228.8 m²   w

_____

Application

Solve.

9. Find the area of this parking lot.

All angles are right angles. _____

10.5 m   12 m

6.2 m   3 m   10.5 m

10. Sergio has 200 feet of fencing. He wants to fence in a pen with the greatest possible area for his dog. What dimensions should he make

the pen? _____

AREA OF TRIANGLES

How can you find a way to compute the area of a triangle? Can you discover a formula for the area of a triangle?

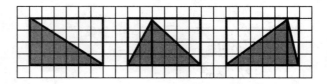

Reminder

The base of a triangle is any one side. The height of a triangle is a line segment from the vertex opposite the base, drawn perpendicular to the base.

Jojo says: Each rectangle is 4 units by 6 units, or 24 square units. I shaded in the triangles. I noticed that the shaded parts are the same size and shape as the non-shaded parts. So each triangle covers $\frac{1}{2}$ the area of the rectangle, or 12 units. Since A (rectangle) = *lw*, the area of a triangle within a rectangle is $\frac{1}{2}$ of *lw*, or

$$A \text{ (triangle)} = \frac{1}{2} lw$$

Salvador says: The dimensions of the triangle are *base (b)* and *height (h)*. So the area of a triangle is $\frac{1}{2}$ of the product of its base times its height.

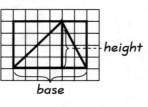

$$A \ (triangle) = \frac{1}{2}(b \times h) \ or \ \frac{1}{2}bh$$

Guided Practice

Reminder

The symbol ∟ is used to indicate that two lines form right angles and are therefore perpendicular.

Reminder

A square measuring 1 centimeter by 1 centimeter is 1 square centimeter, or 1 cm². When you multiply measures of length, the product must be written in terms of square units.

Use this formula for the area of a triangle: $A = \frac{1}{2} bh$.

1. What is the area of this triangle?

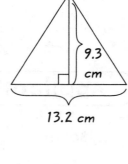

   a. The base is _____ cm.

   The height is _____ cm.

   b. The product of $b \times h$ is

   _____ cm².

   c. To find $\frac{1}{2}$ of the product,

   multiply $\frac{1}{2} \times$ _____.

   d. The area of the triangle is _____ cm².

2. What is the height of this triangle?

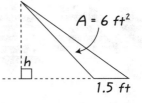

$A = 6\ ft^2$

h

$1.5\ ft$

a. $6\ ft^2 = \frac{1}{2} \times 1.5\ ft \times h$

b. Multiply both sides by 2, since $2 \times \frac{1}{2} = 1$.

$2 \times 6\ ft^2 = \left(2 \times \frac{1}{2}\right) \times 1.5\ ft \times h$

c. $12\ ft^2 = 1.5\ ft \times h$

d. Divide both sides by 1.5. $(12 \div 1.5)\ ft = h$

e. _____ $= h$

Exercises

Find the area of the triangle using the formula $A = \frac{1}{2}\ bh$.

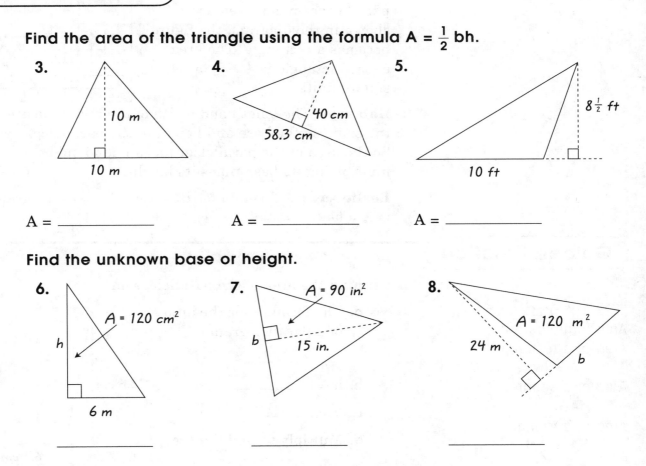

3.

10 m

10 m

A = _____

4.

40 cm

58.3 cm

A = _____

5.

$8\frac{1}{2}\ ft$

10 ft

A = _____

Find the unknown base or height.

6.

h

$A = 120\ cm^2$

6 m

_____

7.

$A = 90\ in.^2$

b

15 in.

_____

8.

$A = 120\ m^2$

24 m

b

_____

Application

9. The height of the triangular mainsail on John's boat is 24 ft. The base along the boom is 12 ft. What is the area of the mainsail?

_____

AREA OF PARALLELOGRAMS

Reminder

A parallelogram has two pairs of parallel sides.

How can you find the area of a parallelogram? What is a formula for the area of a parallelogram?

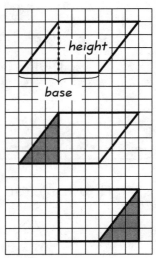

Leslie says: The base of this parallelogram is 6 units. The height is 4 units.

If the triangular part of the parallelogram is moved as shown in the diagram, the figure becomes a rectangle. The area of the rectangle is 4 × 6, or 24 square units.

Bob says: The length and width of the rectangle are the same as the base and height of the parallelogram. So the area of the parallelogram can be found by multiplying its base times its height.

Leslie says: A formula for the area of a parallelogram is $A = bh$.

Guided Practice

Reminder

Area formulas:
Area of a rectangle:
$$A = lw$$
Area of a square:
$$A = s^2$$
Area of a triangle:
$$A = \frac{1}{2}bh$$

1. Find the area of the parallelogram.

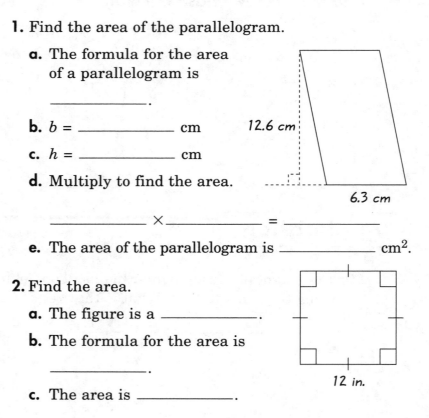

   a. The formula for the area of a parallelogram is

   _____.

   b. $b =$ _____ cm

   c. $h =$ _____ cm

   d. Multiply to find the area.

   _____ × _____ = _____

   e. The area of the parallelogram is _____ cm².

2. Find the area.

   a. The figure is a _____.

   b. The formula for the area is

   _____.

   c. The area is _____.

Exercises

Find the area of each parallelogram.

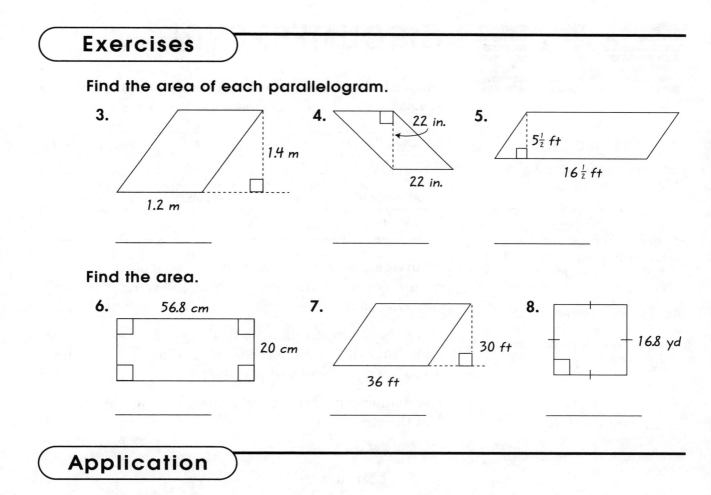

3. 1.4 m   1.2 m

4. 22 in.   22 in.

5. $5\frac{1}{2}$ ft $16\frac{1}{2}$ ft

_____   _____   _____

Find the area.

6. 56.8 cm   20 cm

7. 30 ft   36 ft

8. 16.8 yd

_____   _____   _____

Application

9. How many parallelograms can you draw that have an area of 24 square units? Can you use a pattern? Show your work on graph paper.

Mr. Williams creates fabric designs. Find the area of the shaded region of each design.

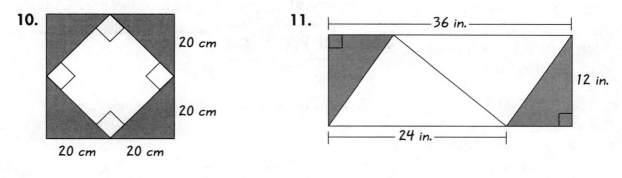

10. 20 cm   20 cm   20 cm   20 cm

11. 36 in.   12 in.   24 in.

_____   _____

CIRCUMFERENCE

Ginger measured the **circumference** and **diameter** of some objects with circular shapes. She made this table.

Object	C	d	Ratio of C to d
Tuna can	$10\frac{3}{4}$ in.	$3\frac{3}{8}$ in.	$3\frac{5}{27}$, or 3.18
Half-dollar	10 cm	3.2 cm	3.13
Baseball	22 cm	7 cm	$\frac{22}{7}$, or 3.14

By dividing, Ginger found that the ratio of circumference to diameter is about the same. For all circles, $\frac{C}{d}$ is about $\frac{22}{7}$, or 3.14. This ratio is called π (pi).

Since the value of this ratio is always the same, you can find either the circumference or the diameter of a circle if you know the value of just one.

The diameter of this sign is 12 inches. How can Ginger find the circumference?

$C = \pi d$

$d = 12$ inches

$\pi \approx 3.14$

$C \approx 3.14 \times 12$

$C \approx 37.68$

The circumference of the sign is about 37.68 inches.

Vocabulary

circumference (C): the distance around a circle

diameter (d): a line segment that passes through the center of a circle and whose endpoints lie on a circle. The length of the segment is also called the diameter.

pi: the Greek letter π that stands for the ratio of the circumference of any circle to its diameter.

$$\pi = \frac{C}{d}$$

The relationship of the circumference of a circle to its diameter can also be expressed by an equivalent sentence:

$C = \pi \times d$, or $C = \pi d$

Reminder

The symbol $\approx$ means "approximately equal to." Any arithmetic operation involving π, which is an approximate value, results in an approximate value.

Reminder

Use $\frac{22}{7}$ or 3.14 for π, depending on whether it is easier to compute a problem with fractions or decimals.

Reminder

Circumference can be estimated by multiplying diameter by 3.

Guided Practice

Use $C = \pi d$. Let $\pi \approx 3.14$, or $\pi \approx \frac{22}{7}$.

1. Find the diameter of the garbage can.

   a. $C = \pi d$

   b. The circumference of the garbage can is

   _____ in.

   c. $\pi \approx$ _____.

   d. $d =$ _____ $\div$ _____

   e. The diameter of the garbage can is about _____ in.

C = 66 in.

Exercises

Use 3.14 or $\frac{22}{7}$ for π, or use the π key on your calculator. If necessary, round answers to the nearest tenth.

Find the circumference of each plate.

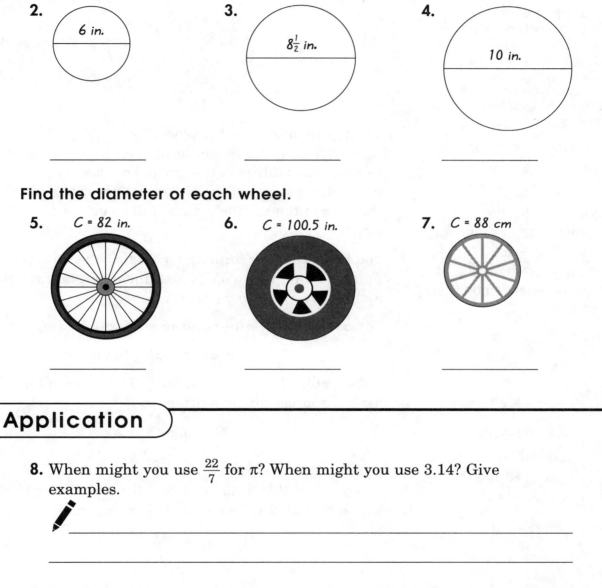

2.

6 in.

_____

3.

$8\frac{1}{2}$ in.

_____

4.

10 in.

_____

Find the diameter of each wheel.

5. C = 82 in.

_____

6. C = 100.5 in.

_____

7. C = 88 cm

_____

Application

8. When might you use $\frac{22}{7}$ for π? When might you use 3.14? Give examples.

_____

_____

9. The diameter of Rosa's bicycle tire is 27 in. About how many times will her tire rotate if she bicycles 1 mile? _____

10. What is the distance around this track? (Hint: The ends are half-circles.)

_____

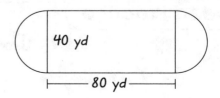

40 yd

├──── 80 yd ────┤

AREA OF A CIRCLE

Vocabulary

radius (r): a line segment with endpoints on the center of a circle and on the circumference. The length of the segment is also called the radius. The radius of a circle is one-half of its diameter.

$$r = \frac{d}{2}, \text{ or } d = 2r$$

Reminder

The formula for the circumference of a circle is:

$$C = \pi d$$

Since d = 2r, the value of the circumference can also be written:

$$C = \pi \times 2r$$

Reminder

When you multiply a number by itself, you square it: $r \times r = r^2$.

Mei-yu cut out a circle, folded it in half, then folded it in half again and again. She cut the 16 pieces apart and arranged them as shown. How can Mei-yu use this rearrangement to find the area of the circle?

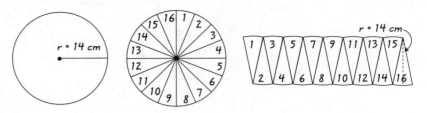

The figure formed by the pieces looks like a parallelogram. The height of the parallelogram is the same as the **radius** of the circle. The base of the parallelogram is $\frac{1}{2}$ of the circumference of the circle. So the area of the parallelogram is the same as that of the circle.

You know that the formula for finding the area of a parallelogram is A = *bh*. Now think about how the base and height relate to a circle.

$$b = \tfrac{1}{2} \times circle,\ or\ \pi r$$

$$h = radius\ of\ circle,\ or\ r$$

Substitute values for *b* and for *h*. The formula for the area of a circle can be written:

$$A = \pi r \times r$$

$$A = \pi r^2$$

Mei-yu used this formula to find the area of her circle. She substituted values for π and for her radius.

$$A = \tfrac{22}{7} \times 14 \times 14$$

$$A = \tfrac{22}{7}(196)$$

$$A = 22(28),\ or\ 616$$

The area of Mei-yu's circle is about 616 cm^2.

Guided Practice

Use $A = \pi r^2$.

1. Find the area of the circular stained-glass window.

   a. The diameter of the window is _____ in.

b. The radius is one-half of the diameter, so the radius of the window is _____ in.

c. To square the radius, multiply _____ × _____.

d. $A \approx 3.14 \times$ _____

e. The area of the stained glass window is _____ in².

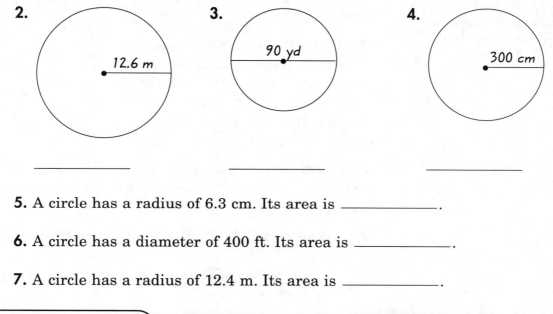

20 in.

Use $A = \pi r^2$ to find the area.

Use $\frac{22}{7}$ or 3.14 for π, or use the pi key on your calculator. When necessary, round answers to the nearest hundredth.

2.

12.6 m

_____

3.

90 yd

_____

4.

300 cm

_____

5. A circle has a radius of 6.3 cm. Its area is _____.

6. A circle has a diameter of 400 ft. Its area is _____.

7. A circle has a radius of 12.4 m. Its area is _____.

8. Ms. Rossi is a mason. She is going to pave the walkway around this circular garden. What is the area of the section she will pave? _____

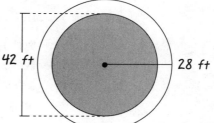

42 ft   28 ft

9. If the diameter of a circle is the same measure as the side of a square, which will have the greater area? How do you know?

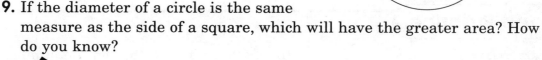

_____

_____

DISTANCE ON THE NUMBER LINE

Vocabulary

integers: the whole numbers (0, +1, +2, +3, etc.) and their negative opposites (0, -1, -2, -3, etc.)

coordinate: a number that corresponds to a point or position on the number line

distance or difference: the value between two coordinates on a number line, without respect to the direction of change

Sometimes it is useful to measure distance or another quantity in two directions. For example, people measure temperature both above and below 0, the freezing point of water on the Celsius scale. To tell values in one direction from values in the other direction, you can use positive and negative numbers called **integers**. Integers can be used to describe:

- a **coordinate** or position on a number line or other scale
- a change in position from one coordinate to another
- a **distance** or **difference** between two coordinates

Problem 1: In one 24-hour period the temperature went from 10°C to -15°C, or 15° below 0. What was the change in temperature?

The change was -25, that is, the temperature fell 25 degrees. Notice that to solve this problem, you must show the *direction of change*—from higher to lower—using a negative integer.

Problem 2: One month the temperature reached a high of 20°C and a low of -10°C. What was the difference between the high and low temperatures?

20° is 30° away from -10°, so the difference was 30°. Neither a positive nor a negative sign is used in this answer because the direction of change is not asked for, only the distance or difference between coordinates.

Temperature Celsius

Guided Practice

Reminder

When using an integer to show direction of change, remember to use a plus (+) or minus (–) sign.

1. Find the distance from A to B on the number line.

a. The coordinate of point A is _____

b. The coordinate of point B is _____

c. The difference between points A and B is _____

d. The distance is _____

2. If a value changes from C to D, what is the change in value?

  a. The direction of change is positive.

  b. The distance from C to D is _____

  c. The change in value is ⁺7.

Exercises

Write an integer to describe the change.

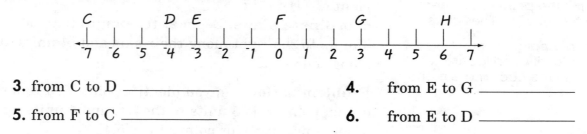

3. from C to D _____

4. from E to G _____

5. from F to C _____

6. from E to D _____

Write an integer to describe the distance between the points with the coordinates given.

7. ⁻12 and 17

8. 72 and 39

9. ⁻19 and ⁻66

_____

_____

_____

10. 5 and 64

11. ⁻20 and 8

12. 16 and ⁻24

_____

_____

_____

Application

13. If Marquell bought a television for $499, and then sold it the next year for $220 dollars, what was the television's change in value? What is the difference between the two prices?

_____

_____

14. One day, the temperature in Madison, Wisconsin, dropped from a high of ⁻2°C to a low of ⁻8°C. What was the change from the high to the low temperature? What was the difference?

_____

THE COORDINATE PLANE: GRAPHING POINTS

Vocabulary

coordinate plane: two perpendicular number lines that cut a plane into four regions

axis: the horizontal number line in a coordinate plane is called the *x*-axis. The vertical number line is called the *y*-axis.

origin: the point (0,0) where the two number lines cross

ordered pair: two numbers that identify and locate a point in the coordinate plane

An **ordered pair** gives the (*x*,*y*) coordinates of a point. The first number tells how far and in which direction to move on the *x*-**axis.** The second number tells how to move on the *y*-axis.

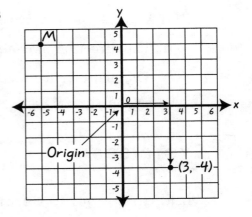

Problem 1: Locate point (3,⁻4) on the **coordinate plane.** Begin at the **origin** (0,0). Move 3 units to the right along the *x*-axis and ⁻4 units (down) along the *y*-axis.

Problem 2: How can you identify point M? From the origin, point M is 5 units to the left and 4 units up. The ordered pair (*x*,*y*) for point M is (⁻5,4).

Guided Practice

Reminder

If an integer does not have a sign, assume that it is positive.

Reminder

To graph or locate a point on the coordinate plane, begin at the origin, (0,0).

1. Give the ordered pair for point P.

    a. From the origin, P is _____ units left.

    b. P is _____ units down.

    c. The ordered pair for point P is (_____).

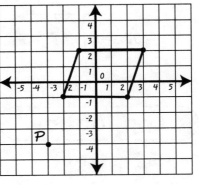

2. Locate the points (3,2), (2,⁻1), (⁻2,⁻1), and (⁻1,2). Connect the points in order. What is the figure?

    a. To locate (3,2), move 3 units _____ and 2 units _____.

    b. To locate (2,⁻1), move 2 units _____ and 1 unit _____.

c. To locate (⁻2,⁻1), move 2 units _____ and 1

unit _____ .

d. To locate (⁻1,2), move 1 unit _____ and 2 units

_____ .

e. Connect the points in order. The figure is a _____ .

Exercises

Graph each point on the coordinate plane. Connect the points in order. What is the figure?

3. (⁻5,0)   **4.** (⁻2,0)   **5.** (0,3)

6. (2,0)   **7.** (5,0)   **8.** (2,⁻2)

9. (4,⁻5)   **10.** (0,⁻3)   **11.** (⁻4,⁻5)

12. (⁻2,⁻2)   **13.** (⁻5,0)

14. The figure is a _____ .

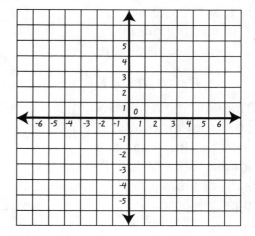

Give the ordered pair for each point.

15. Point K _____

16. Point T _____

17. Point V _____

18. Point W _____

19. Point B _____

20. Point N _____

Application

COOPERATIVE
LEARNING

21. Construct a coordinate plane. Use points to draw an object on your coordinate plane. Then read the coordinates of your points and have a classmate graph your figure on his or her coordinate plane. Exchange roles. Graph the points of your classmate's object on your coordinate plane.

THE COORDINATE PLANE: DRAWING FIGURES

Reminder

A right triangle has one right angle. An equilateral triangle has three equal sides. An isosceles triangle has two equal sides. A scalene triangle has all sides different lengths.

Reminder

The Pythagorean theorem says that for a right triangle, the square of the longest side is equal to the sum of the squares of the other sides.

$$c^2 = a^2 + b^2$$

How can you classify triangle *ABC*?

Carol says: Since the axes are perpendicular, they cut triangle *ABC* into two right triangles. The coordinate plane shows that the short sides of these right triangles are 4 and 3 units long.

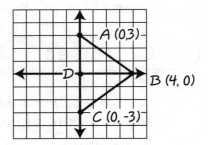

Arnold says: You can use the Pythagorean theorem to find the third sides of these two right triangles: segments *AB* and *BC*.

$$c^2 = a^2 + b^2$$

$$c^2 = 3^2 + 4^2 \quad \longleftarrow \quad \text{Substitute known values}$$

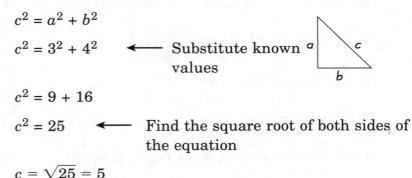

$$c^2 = 9 + 16$$

$$c^2 = 25 \quad \longleftarrow \quad \text{Find the square root of both sides of the equation}$$

$$c = \sqrt{25} = 5$$

The long sides of the right triangles are 5 units long. These are two sides of triangle *ABC*. So triangle *ABC* is isosceles.

Guided Practice

Reminder

The first coordinate of an ordered pair (x,y) shows direction and distance on the horizontal (x) axis. The second coordinate shows direction and distance on the vertical (y) axis.

1. What type of triangle is this? Explain your reasoning.

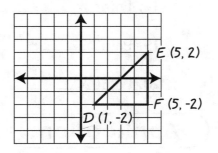

a. The axes and grid lines of a coordinate plane are

perpendicular

b. Angle *F* of triangle *DEF* is a _____ angle.

c. The length of side *DF* is _____ units long.

d. The length of side *EF* is _____ units long.

e. Sides *DF* and *EF* are _____*equal*_____.

f. A triangle with two equal sides and a right angle is _____.

What type of triangle is shown on the coordinate plane? Explain your reasoning.

2. _____
_____
_____
_____
_____

3. _____
_____
_____
_____
_____

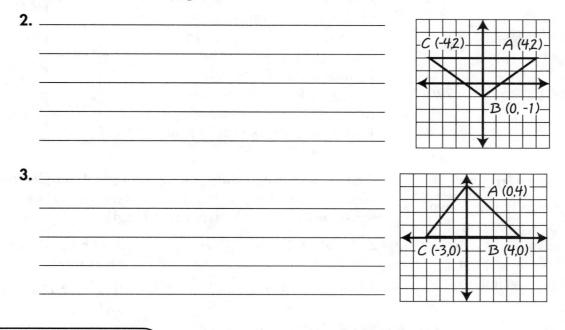

4. Set up a coordinate plane. Draw an isosceles right triangle on the plane. Label the points. Explain how you determined the triangle to be isosceles right.

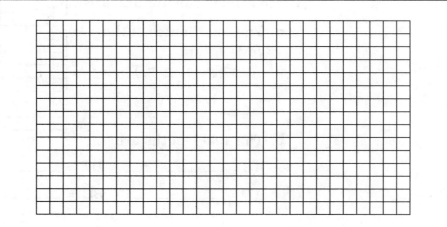

THE COORDINATE PLANE: FINDING PERIMETERS AND AREAS

9•9

Reminder

Some useful formulas:

Square:
  Area: $A = s^2$
  Perimeter: $P = 4s$

Rectangle:
  Area: $A = lw$
  Perimeter: $P = 2l + 2w$

Reminder

The distance between two points, or length of a line segment, is a positive number given without respect to direction.

How can you find the perimeter and area of this figure?

Luis Rosa says: I can draw grid lines through the vertices, or corners, of the figure to make four right triangles. The hypotenuses of the right triangles form the sides of the figure. Can we use the Pythagorean theorem to find these side lengths?

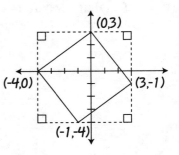

Ben Rosen says: Sure, all of the right triangles have shorter sides 3 units and 4 units long. So all the hypotenuses must be the same length.

$c^2 = a^2 + b^2$ Pythagorean theorem

$c^2 = 9 + 16 = 25$ Substitute known values.

$c = \sqrt{25}$, or 5   Find square root of both sides.

The figure is a square with sides 5 units in length.

Perimeter = $4s = 4 \times 5$, or 20 units.

Area = $s^2 = 5^2$, or 25 square units.

Guided Practice

1. Find the perimeter and area.

   a. The coordinates of the vertices are

   A ($^-$4,$^-$1); B (2,$^-$1);

   C (2, 3); D ($^-$4, 3).

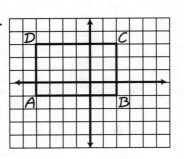

   b. The side lengths are:

   AB = _____   DC = _____

   AD = _____   BC = _____

c. The figure is a _____ with sides of length _____ and _____.

d. The perimeter is _____ and the area is _____.

Find the perimeter and area of each figure.

2. The coordinates are _____.

The area is _____.

The perimeter is _____.

3. The coordinates are _____.

The area is _____.

The perimeter is _____.

4. The coordinates are _____.

The area is _____.

The perimeter is _____.

5. The coordinates are _____.

The area is _____.

The perimeter is _____.

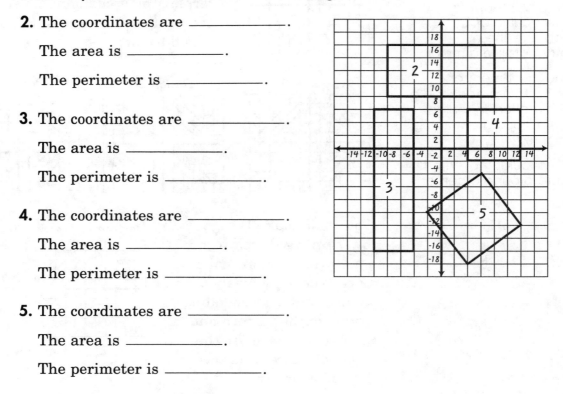

Application

The following questions refer to points on the coordinate plane.

6. Use examples to show how to find the distance between two points with the same *y*-value.

_____

_____

7. Use examples to show how to find the distance between two points with the same *x*-value.

_____

_____

SLIDES, FLIPS, AND TURNS

Vocabulary

flip: the movement of a figure over a line of symmetry. The line of symmetry acts like a mirror.

slide: the movement of a figure a certain distance in a certain direction. In a slide there is no flipping or turning of the figure.

turn: the circular movement of a figure around a center point.

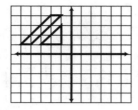

Ted drew this pattern on a coordinate plane. How could you move this same pattern, without changing its shape or size, to make Designs A, B, and C as shown below?

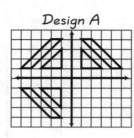 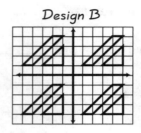 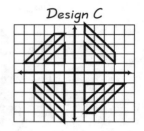

Design A   *Design B*   *Design C*

You could make Design A by **flipping** the pattern once over the x-axis and once over the y-axis. Notice that corresponding points of the pattern and its mirror image are the same distance from the line of symmetry.

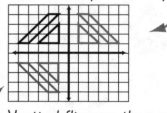

Horizontal flip over the y-axis

Vertical flip over the x-axis

You could **slide** the pattern in three different directions to make Design B. Notice that in a slide each point of the figure moves exactly the same distance in the same direction.

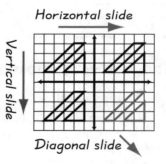

Horizontal slide

Vertical slide

Diagonal slide

You could **turn** the pattern in a circular motion around the origin to make Design C.

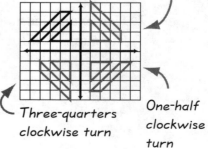

One-quarter clockwise turn

One-half clockwise turn

Three-quarters clockwise turn

Reminder

Vertices are the points, or corners, where sides of polygons meet.

1. Look at the parallelograms in Design A. Compare the coordinates of corresponding vertices. Complete the table. Look for a pattern.

Parallelogram		
Vertex	**Flip over the x-axis**	**Flip over the y-axis**
(−1,4)	(−1,−4)	(1,4)
(−2,4)	(−2,−4)	
(−5,1)	(−5,−1)	
(−4,1)	(−4,−1)	

2. The coordinates for corresponding vertices of the triangle in Design A are given in the table. Find the coordinates for the flips of the triangle without looking at the design. Use what you observed in Exercise 1.

Triangle		
Vertex	**Flip over the x-axis**	**Flip over the y-axis**
(−1,1)		
(−3,1)		
(−1,3)		

3. Flip this pattern over the x-axis and over the y-axis to make a design.

a. To flip a point over the x-axis, use the same x value and change the sign of the _____ value.

b. To flip a point over the y-axis, change the sign of the x value and use the same _____ value.

Exercises

Use the parallelograms in Ted's clockwise turn design, Design C. Compare coordinates of corresponding vertices. Complete the table.

4.

Parallelogram			
Pattern	$\frac{1}{4}$-Turn	$\frac{1}{2}$-Turn	$\frac{3}{4}$-Turn
(−1,4)	(4,1)	(1,−4)	(−4,−1)
(−2,4)	(4,2)		
(−5,1)	(1,5)		
(−4,1)	(1,4)		

The coordinates for the vertices of the triangles in Design C are given in the table. Find the coordinates for the clockwise turns of the triangle without looking at the design. Use what you observed in Exercise 4.

5.

Triangle			
Pattern	$\frac{1}{4}$-Turn	$\frac{1}{2}$-Turn	$\frac{3}{4}$-Turn
(−1,1)			
(−3,1)			
(−1,3)			

Complete the statement.

6. To turn a point $\frac{1}{4}$-turn clockwise about the origin: change the

_____ of the x-value and use it as the _____ value; and

change the _____ value to x.

7. To turn a point $\frac{1}{2}$-turn clockwise about the origin: change the

_____ of the x-value and the _____ of the y value.

8. Turn the pattern $\frac{1}{4}$-, $\frac{1}{2}$-, and $\frac{3}{4}$-turn clockwise about the origin to make a design.

9. Slide the pattern horizontally, vertically, and diagonally to make a design.

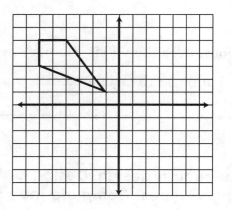

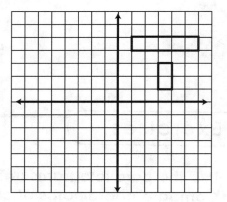

10. Study the vertical and horizontal slides of the triangle in Design B on page 62. Make up and check rules for changing the coordinates of points in a figure to create a slide pattern.

_____

_____

11. Draw a geometric pattern in one quarter of the coordinate plane. Use slides, flips, or turns to create a design. You may want to cut out or trace your pattern to experiment with designs. List the movements you use to create your design.

_____

_____

_____

_____

12. Use drawings or cut-out patterns to compare $\frac{1}{4}$-, $\frac{1}{2}$-, and $\frac{3}{4}$-clockwise turns with $\frac{1}{4}$-, $\frac{1}{2}$-, and $\frac{3}{4}$-counterclockwise turns. Explain your findings.

_____

_____

_____

_____

Which is more? Circle your answer.

1. 3 ft or 30 in.

2. 10.5 ft or 4 yd

3. 14 c or 3 qt

4. 2.5 gal or 16 pt

5. 870 lb or 0.5 T

6. 100 oz or 6 lb

Change each measurement.

7. 60 in. = _____ ft

8. 10 ft = _____ yd

9. 4 lb = _____ oz

10. 1.2 T = _____ lb

11. 7 qt = _____ c

12. 15 pt = _____ qt

Use the 1.5-inch line as a unit to estimate the line length in exercises 13–17.

1.5 inches

13. ├──────┤

_____

14. ├────┤

15. ├──────────────────────────────┤

_____   _____

16. ├──────────┤

17. ├────────────────────┤

_____   _____

18. Mai Lu made 8 gallons of apple sauce. How many 1-pint jars can she fill? _____

19. The length of Leon's stride is 30 inches. How many steps will he take to walk the 60 yards across a hockey field? _____

5-8 CUMULATIVE REVIEW

Which is more? Circle your answer.

1. 12 m or 20,000 cm

2. 6000 m or 5.8 km

3. 18 L or 180 cL

4. 400 mL or 4 L

5. 3.3 mg or 0.3 g

6. 0.07 kg or 7 g

Change the unit of measure.

7. 15,200 m = _____ km

8. 28 cm = _____ m

9. 900 mL = _____ L

10. 50 cL = _____ mL

11. 9300 g = _____ kg

12. 6.2 g = _____ mg

Use the 3-cm line as a unit to estimate the length.

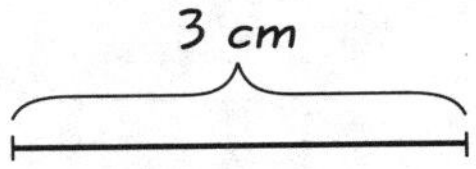

3 cm

13. ├───────────────────────────┤

_____

14. ├─────────────────────────────────────┤

_____

15. ├──────┤

16. ├────┤

17. ├───────────┤

_____

_____

_____

Match each prefix with its value.

18. milli-

a. 1000

19. kilo-

b. 0.001 or $\frac{1}{1000}$

20. centi-

c. 0.01 or $\frac{1}{100}$

9-12 CUMULATIVE REVIEW

Draw a sketch to illustrate each term.

1. Ray

2. Parallel lines

3. Perpendicular lines

4. Line segment

Find the measure of each angle and classify it as right, acute, or obtuse.

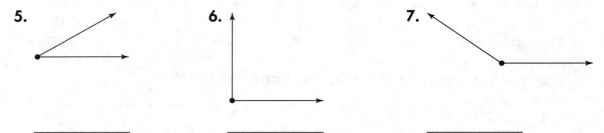

5. _____

6. _____

7. _____

Find the missing angle measurement for each triangle.

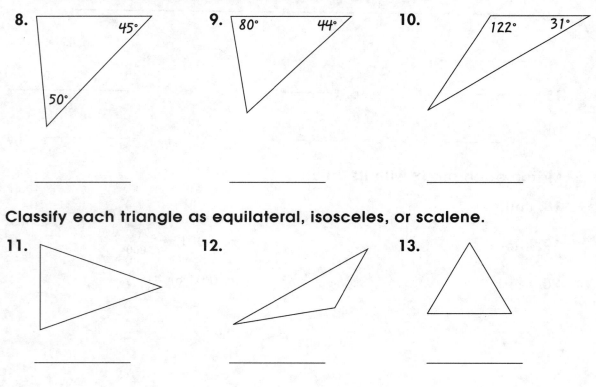

8. _____

9. _____

10. _____

Classify each triangle as equilateral, isosceles, or scalene.

11. _____

12. _____

13. _____

13-16 CUMULATIVE REVIEW

Find the measure of angle b. The triangle in Exercise 2 is equilateral.

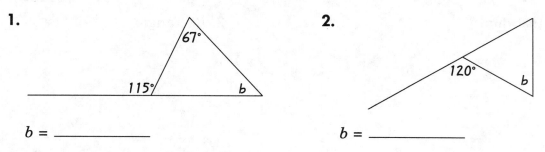

1.

b = _____

2.

b = _____

Write *congruent*, *similar*, or *neither* for each pair of triangles.

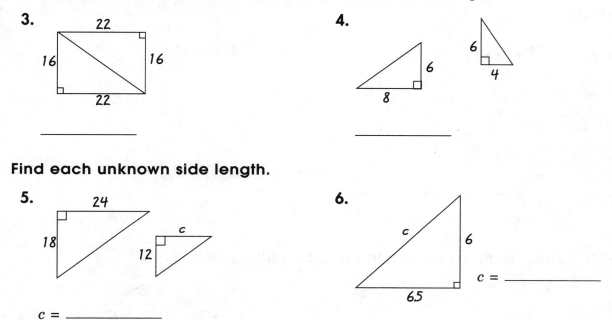

3.

_____

4.

_____

Find each unknown side length.

5.

c = _____

6.

c = _____

7. Wendy is 64 inches tall. One day her shadow was 48 inches long at the same time her sister's shadow was 30 inches long. How tall is Wendy's

sister? _____

8. If you know the measure of an interior angle, how can you find the measure of its exterior angle?

_____

_____

Draw an example of each quadrilateral. Then describe its sides, angles, and diagonals.

1. Square

_____

_____

_____

2. Rectangle

_____

_____

_____

3. Parallelogram

_____

_____

_____

4. Rhombus

_____

_____

_____

Find the measure of B in each quadrilateral.

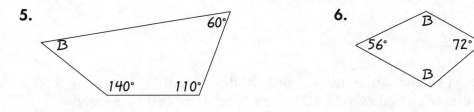

5.

_____

6.

_____

List all of the quadrilaterals that fit each description.

7. Has exactly one pair of parallel sides _____

8. Has two different pairs of congruent sides _____

9. Has perpendicular diagonals _____

CUMULATIVE REVIEW

Find the perimeter of each figure.

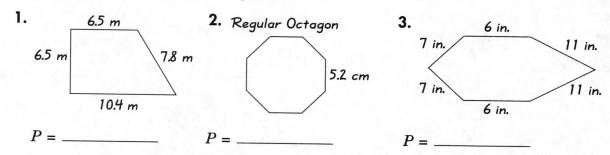

1.
6.5 m
6.5 m
7.8 m
10.4 m

P = _____

2. Regular Octagon

5.2 cm

P = _____

3.
6 in.
7 in.   11 in.
7 in.   11 in.
6 in.

P = _____

Find the area of each figure.

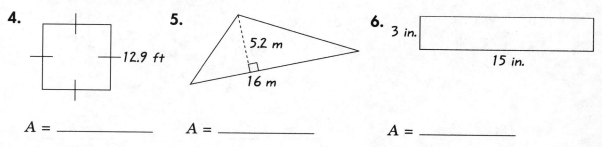

4.
12.9 ft

A = _____

5.
5.2 m
16 m

A = _____

6.
3 in.
15 in.

A = _____

Find the unknown length for each figure.

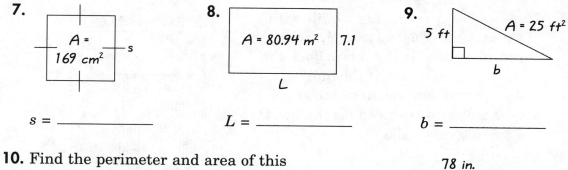

7.
A = 169 cm²
s

s = _____

8.
A = 80.94 m²   7.1
L

L = _____

9.
5 ft   A = 25 ft²
b

b = _____

10. Find the perimeter and area of this
computer work station. Explain how you
solved for each.

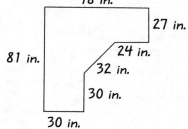

78 in.
27 in.
81 in.
24 in.
32 in.
30 in.
30 in.

_____

_____

_____

_____

23-25 CUMULATIVE REVIEW

Find the area of each quadrilateral.

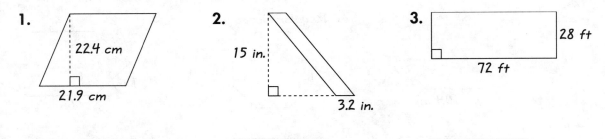

1.

22.4 cm

21.9 cm

_____

2.

15 in.

3.2 in.

_____

3.

28 ft

72 ft

_____

Find the circumference and area of each circle.

4.

12.6 m

_____

_____

5.

40 ft

_____

_____

6.

9 cm

_____

_____

7. Ms. Webster is making a quilt with squares like the one shown. How much of each type of fabric does she need for a square? If the quilt has 48 squares, how much of each type of fabric does she need for the quilt? Complete the table.

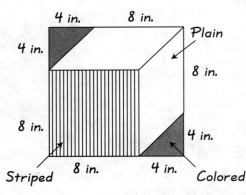

4 in.   8 in.

Plain

4 in.

8 in.

8 in.

Striped

8 in.   4 in.

4 in.

Colored

Fabric Needed		
	For each square	For the quilt
Plain		
Striped		
Colored		

Plot these points on the coordinate plane.

1. (⁻5, 4)   **3.** (4, ⁻3)

2. (⁻5, ⁻3)   **4.** (4, 4)

Connect the points in order.

5. The figure is a _____

6. Its perimeter is _____ units.

7. Its area is _____ square units.

8. What type of triangle is shown on the coordinate plane? Explain how you know.

_____
_____
_____
_____

9. Flip the triangle across the *y*-axis. What are the coordinates of the points?

_____

10. Flip the triangle across the *x*-axis. What are the coordinates of the points?

_____

11. Turn the triangle $\frac{1}{2}$-turn clockwise about the origin. What are the coordinates of the points?

_____

12. Turning the triangle $\frac{1}{2}$-turn clockwise about the origin is the same as flipping the triangle over the _____-axis and then flipping it again over the _____-axis.

ANSWER KEY

LESSON 1 (pages 2–3)
   1. a. 12 **b.** divide **c.** $1\frac{1}{4}$ **d.** $1\frac{1}{4}$ **3.** 8 **5.** 327
   7. 0.2 **9.** 5632 **11.** 99 **13.** 50 **15.** 175
   17. Answers will vary.

LESSON 2 (pages 4–5)
   1. a. his hand **b.** 8 inches **c.** 3.5 hand spans
   d. 28
   3. 36 ft **5.** 2 ft **7.** $\frac{1}{2}$ in. **9.** 5 in. **11.** 27 in.
   13. Estimating units will vary.

LESSON 3 (pages 6–7)
   1. a. 4 **b.** multiply **c.** 10 **d.** 10
   3. 8 **5.** 1 **7.** $\frac{1}{2}$ **9.** 1 **11.** 28 oz
   13. 15 pt **15.** $1\frac{1}{2}$ c **17.** 4 gal
   19. 16 **21.** no, 8 oz more

LESSON 4 (pages 8–9)
   1. a. none **b.** 80 ounces, 4 pounds **c.** 4 ounces
   3. 24 lb **5.** 9.5 oz **7.** 36
   9. 4 **11.** 0.4 **13.** 83,200
   15. Answers will vary. Art might know the baby
   is lighter than he is and lighter than his
   bicycle, a little lighter than his dog, heavier
   than his jacket or his toothbrush.

LESSON 5 (pages 10–11)
   1. a. 100 **b.** multiply **c.** 340
   3. 50,000 **5.** 28.9 **7.** 0.462
   9. m **11.** km **13.** 71
   15. Answers will vary. 1 km = 1000 m
   = 100,000 cm, 1 m = 100 cm.

LESSON 6 (pages 12–13)
   1. a. $2\frac{1}{2}$ **b.** 10 **c.** 10
   3. 5 cm **5.** 12 cm **7.** 423 m

LESSON 7 (pages 14–15)
   1. a. 10 **b.** multiply **c.** 100 **d.** $500 **e.** $500
   3. centiliter **5.** centiliter
   7. 5 **9.** 3620 **11.** 7100 **13.** 15, $39.50

LESSON 8 (pages 16–17)
   1. a. 200 milligrams **b.** 200 kilograms
   c. 200 grams
   3. 1.1 kg **5.** 125 mg **7.** 0.0083 **9.** 57
   11. 7.002 **13.** 27 **15.** 16

LESSON 9 (pages 18–19)
   1. a. parallel lines **b.** the sides of the ruler
   3. f. **5.** e. **7.** a.
   9. Perspective involves drawing objects in the
   foreground larger and those in the back-
   ground smaller to give the appearance of
   depth. This process distorts actual measurements to preserve the visual image.
   11. Students should identify line segments,
   points, parallel and perpendicular lines.

LESSON 10 (pages 20–21)
   1. a. 20°, 33°, 127° **b.** acute, acute, obtuse
   Answers for Exercises 2–14 may vary slightly.
   3. 110°, obtuse **5.** 76°, acute **7.** 180°, straight
   9. 125°, obtuse **11.** 80°, acute
   13. Right angle, 90°; Acute angle, less than 90°;
   Obtuse angle, greater than 90°; Straight
   angle, 180°; Examples will vary.

LESSON 11 (pages 22–23)
   1. a. 72 **b.** 72 **c.** 36 **d.** 72 + 72 + 36 = 180
   3. 45°, 45°, 90°, 180°
   5. 108°, 40°, 32°, 180°

LESSON 12 (pages 24–25)
   1. a. 0 **b.** scalene **c.** 98°, 25°, 57° **d.** 0 **e.** no
   3. Isosceles, 2, 2, 1
   5. Isosceles, 2, 2, 0
   7. An equilateral triangle has three 60°
   angles, it cannot be a right triangle.
   9. A scalene triangle can be a right triangle,
   examples will vary.

LESSON 13 (pages 26–27)
   1. a. 120 **b.** 60 **c.** the two angles that are not
   next to the exterior angle **d.** 60 and 60
   3. 150°, 30°, 45° and 105°
   5. The exterior angle is equal to the sum of
   the two remote interior angles.
   7. Since the sum of the angles of a triangle is
   180° and an angle and its exterior angle
   form a straight angle with a measure of
   180°, the remote interior angles must be the
   same as the measure of the exterior angle.

LESSON 14 (pages 28–29)
   1. a. 1.5 cm, 3 cm, 2.3 cm **b.** 1.8 cm, 3 cm, 2.6
   cm **c.** 108°, 26°, 46° **d.** 87°, 37°, 56°
   e. 0 **f.** 1 **g.** no
   3. 3, 3, yes **5.** 3, 0, no
   7. There is only one.

LESSON 15
   (pages 30–31)
   1. a. $\frac{6}{8}, \frac{4}{7}$ **b.** $\frac{6}{8}, \frac{4}{7}$ **c.** No
   3. $\frac{15}{8}, \frac{5}{3}$, the triangles are not similar.
   5. m = 24

LESSON 16 (pages 32–35)
   1. d. 4 **e.** 5.2 **f.** 27.04 **g.** 27.04 **h.** yes

3. 5 cm, 12 cm, 13 cm, Yes.   **5.** 17   **7.** 48
9. The sum of the squares of two sides of a right triangle is equal to the square of the longest side.
11. No. Examples will vary. Sample: For an equilateral triangle with sides 6 inches, the sum of the squares of no two sides is equal to the square of the third side.
13. 20 inches

LESSON 17 (pages 36–37)
   1. a. 1 inch **b.** Yes **c.** 1.25 inches **d.** Yes
   3. b. square   **5.** Yes, Yes   **7.** Yes, Yes
   9. Yes, Yes

LESSON 18 (pages 38–39)
1.

	Kite	Trapezoid	Rhombus	Parallelogram
diagonals are congruent				
diagonals bisect each other			✓	✓
diagonals are perpendicular	✓		✓	
diagonals bisect the angles			✓	

3–5.

	Rhombus	Parallelogram	Trapezoid	Kite
opposite angles are equal	✓	✓		
adjacent angles are equal				
opposite angles have a sum of 180°				
adjacent angles have a sum of 180°	✓	✓		

LESSON 19 (pages 40–41)
   1. a. 50° **b.** 50° **c.** 130° **d.** 130° **e.** 360°
   3. Rectangle, 360°   **5.** Trapezoid, 360°
   7. The sum of the angles of a quadrilateral is 360°.

LESSON 20 (pages 42–43)
   1. a. $4\frac{1}{2} + 2 + 5\frac{3}{4} + 1\frac{1}{4}$ **b.** 13.5 **c.** 14 **d.** Yes
For 3 to 5, estimates will vary.
   3. $54\frac{5}{6}$ **5.** 174.1   **7.** 42, P = 8s
   9. The perimeter is equal to the number of sides times the length of one side.

LESSON 21 (pages 44–45)
   1. a. square **b.** $A = s^2$ **c.** 25.6 **d.** 655.36
   3. 30.25 ft²   **5.** 13,225 in.²
   7. 10 yd   **9.** 294.9 m²

LESSON 22 (pages 46–47)
   1. a. 13.2, 9.3 **b.** 122.76 **c.** 122.76 **d.** 61.38
   3. 50 m²   **5.** 42.5 ft²   **7.** 12 in   **9.** 144 ft²

LESSON 23 (pages 48–49)
   1. a. $A = bh$ **b.** 6.3 cm **c.** 12.6 cm
      d. 6.3 × 12.6 = 79.38 **e.** 79.38
   3. 1.68 m²   **5.** 90.75 ft²   **7.** 1080 ft²
   9. Answers will vary. Whole number bh combinations are: 1 and 24, 2 and 12, 3 and 8, 4 and 6   **11.** 144 in²

LESSON 24 (pages 50–51)
   1. b. 66 **c.** $\frac{22}{7}$ **d.** 66, $\frac{22}{7}$ **e.** 21
      The answers for the exercises may vary slightly depending upon which value is used for pi.
   3. 26.70 in.   **5.** $26\frac{1}{11}$ in.   **7.** 28 cm
   9. About 747 times

LESSON 25 (pages 52–53)
   1. a. 20 **b.** 10 **c.** 10 × 10 **d.** 100 **e.** 314
      The answers for the exercises may vary slightly depending upon which value students use for pi.
   3. 6358.5 yd²   **5.** 124.63 cm²   **7.** 483 m²
   9. The square, the circle will fit inside the square.

LESSON 26 (pages 54–55)
   1. a. 0 **b.** ⁻5 **c.** 5 **d.** 5
   3. ⁺3   **5.** ⁻7   **7.** 29   **9.** 47
   11. 28   **13.** ⁻$279, $279

LESSON 27 (pages 56–57)
   1. a. 3 **b.** 4 **c.** (-3,-4)
   3–13.

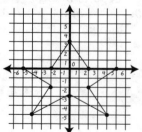

   15. (⁻2,3)   **17.** (⁻3,0)   **19.** (4,2)
   21. Objects will vary.

LESSON 28 (pages 58–59)
   1. b. right **c.** 4 **d.** 4 **f.** isosceles right
   3. Scalene: The points lie along the axes. The length from (0,0) to A is 4 units. The length from (0,0) to B is 4 units. The length from (0,0) to C is 3 units. The lengths of the sides can be found using the Pythagorean

Theorem. All three sides are different lengths, so the triangle is scalene.

LESSON 29 (pages 60–61)
1. b. AB = 6, DC = 6, AD = 4, BC = 4 **c.** rectangle, 6, 4 **d.** 20 units, 24 square units
3. (⁻4,6), (⁻4,⁻16), (⁻10,6), (⁻10,⁻16), 56 units, 132 square units
5. (⁻2,⁻10), (4,⁻18), (12,⁻12), (6,⁻4), 40 units, 100 square units.
7. Examples will vary. Subtract y-values

LESSON 30 (pages 62–65)
1. (2,4), (5,1), (4,1) **3. a.** y **b.** y
5. $\frac{1}{4}$-Turn: (1,1), (1,3), (3,1) $\frac{1}{2}$-Turn: (1,⁻1), (3,⁻1), (1,⁻3) $\frac{3}{4}$-Turn: (⁻1,⁻1), (⁻1,⁻3), (⁻3,⁻1)
7. sign, sign
9. Slide patterns may vary.

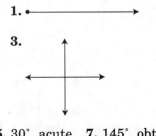

11. Patterns will vary.

CUMULATIVE REVIEW: LESSONS 1–4 (page 66)
1. 3 ft **3.** 14 c **5.** 0.5 T **7.** 5 **9.** 64 **11.** 28
13. $\frac{3}{4}$ in. **15.** $4\frac{1}{2}$ in. **17.** 2 in. **19.** 72

CUMULATIVE REVIEW: LESSONS 5–8 (page 67)
1. 20,000 cm **3.** 18 L **5.** 0.3 g **7.** 15.2
9. 0.9 **11.** 9.3 **13.** 6 cm **15.** 2 cm
17. 3.5 cm **19.** a

CUMULATIVE REVIEW: LESSONS 9–12 (page 68)
1–3. Answers will vary, samples are given.

1.

3.

5. 30°, acute **7.** 145°, obtuse
9. 56° **11.** isosceles
13. equilateral

CUMULATIVE REVIEW: LESSONS 13–16 (page 69)
1. 48° **3.** congruent **5.** 16 **7.** 40 inches

CUMULATIVE REVIEW: LESSONS 17–19 (page 70)
1–3. Drawings will vary.
1. All four sides are congruent, all four angles are 90°, diagonals are congruent and perpendicular
3. Opposite sides are congruent, opposite angles are congruent, diagonals are congruent
5. 50° **7.** Trapezoid
9. Square, rhombus, kite

CUMULATIVE REVIEW: LESSONS 20–22 (page 71)
1. P =31.2 cm **3.** 48 in. **5.** 41.6 m²
7. 13 cm **9.** 10 ft

CUMULATIVE REVIEW: LESSONS 23–25 (page 72)
1. 490.56 cm²
3. 2016 ft²
Answers to Exercises 5–7 may vary depending upon what value of pi students use.
5. C = 251.2 ft, A = 5024 ft²
7. For each square: 64 in.² Plain, 64 in.² Striped, 16 in.² Colored For the quilt: 3072 in.² Plain, 3072 in.² Striped, 768 in.² Colored

CUMULATIVE REVIEW: LESSONS 26–30 (page 73)
1–3.

5. rectangle
7. 63 square units
9. (5,1), (5,5), (2,5)
11. (5,⁻1), (5,⁻5), (2,⁻5)